The Last Economy
A Guide to the Age of Intelligent Economics
Emad Mostaque

Intelligent Internet

© Emad Mostaque, 2025. All rights reserved.

No part of this publication may be reproduced, stored in a retrieval system, or transmitted in any form or by any means—electronic, mechanical, photocopying, recording, or otherwise—without the prior written permission of the author and publisher, except for brief quotations used in reviews, articles, or scholarly works.

All rights reserved worldwide. This book may not be distributed, resold, licensed, translated, adapted, or otherwise exploited in any form or by any means, including electronic, audio, or digital reproduction, without the express written consent of the author or publisher.

The author asserts the moral right to be identified as the author of this work.

This publication is provided for informational purposes only. The author and publisher disclaim any liability arising from its use.

Published by Intelligent Internet (L42 Ltd)
ISBN: 978-1-0369-3411-8
First Edition: 2025

Dedication

To my wife, my compass in shifting tides.

To my children, heirs of the dawn this book strives to usher in.

To all who stood beside me,
your faith and friendship carried me.

And to you who read these words,
may they be seeds you carry forward,
until they bloom in the world you create.

Contents

Introduction   1
The Thousand-Day Window

1. The Intelligence Inversion   6
2. Harbingers of the Storm   12
3. The Seven Fatal Lies of a Dying Paradigm   17
4. The Dashboard for Insanity   24
   GDP and the Meaning Crisis
5. The Trial by Fire   29
6. The Engine of Order   34
   Intelligence Against Entropy
7. The Generative Engine   40
8. The MIND of a Civilization   45
9. The Three Flows   51
   The Blind Scholars and the Elephant
10. The Network Prison   58
11. The Cathedral and the Bazaar 2.0   63
12. Intelligent Game Theory   67
13. The Dual Engine   72
    The Rhythms of Change

14.	The New Social Contract	77
15.	The Alignment Economy Who Commands the Machines?	82
16.	The Three Futures	87
17.	The Symbiotic State Governance as Geometry Engineering	92
18.	Money for Two Worlds	97
19.	The Nucleation of the New A Strategy for Hope	102
20.	Intelligent Macroeconomics	106
21.	After Economics	110

Epilogue   115
The Thousandth Day

Appendix A   119
The Formal Foundations of Intelligence Theory

Appendix B   124
The Generative AI Mirror

Appendix C   128
The MIND Dashboard: A Practitioner's Guide

Appendix D   132
A Lexicon of Intelligent Economics

Bibliography   137

Introduction
The Thousand-Day Window

Your economic life expectancy is shrinking. Not your career. Not your current job. Your entire economic relevance as a human being. We are living through a historical epoch of unprecedented change, a finite window of time during which the fundamental rules of our civilization are being rewritten. This is not speculation. This is a phase transition.

When I write these words, I do so with the peculiar burden of someone who has seen both worlds. For years, I was a macro hedge fund manager. My job was to find the cracks in the global financial system and bet on them before they shattered. I learned to see the world not as economists described it, but as a fragile, interconnected network governed by fear, greed, and the brutal physics of capital flows.

Then I left that world to help build the engine of the next one. As the founder of Stability AI, I've been in the rooms where the mathematics of your obsolescence were calculated. Not through malice, but as an inevitable outcome of optimization. I've watched as artificial intelligence learned to see, to write, to reason, to create. I've seen the training curves that spell doom for every knowledge worker.

Now, I see the system I once exploited from the perspective of the force that will shatter it completely. This book is born from that unique, terrifying vantage point. It is both a diagnosis from an insider and a blueprint from an architect.

But here is what haunts me: we are achieving the greatest triumph in human history, the liberation of intelligence from the constraints of biology, and our economic system can only process it as catastrophe. This is not a theoretical problem. Here's the cosmic joke that would be hilarious if it weren't so tragic. I call it the Abundance Trap: We are about to achieve post-scarcity in the realm of intelligence, and our scarcity-based economic system is going to process this abundance as poverty. Consider the two dashboards by which we measure our world.

The first is the official dashboard of the old economy. The stock market is at an all time high. GDP growth is steady. Unemployment is historically low. By every metric our leaders watch, we have never been more prosperous.

The second is the dashboard of human reality. Life satisfaction is at its lowest point since records began. Deaths of despair from suicide, overdose, and alcoholism are at epidemic levels. A generation is drowning in debt, unable to afford a home or start a family. We are richer on paper and poorer in spirit than at any point in modern history.

This disconnect is the first siren of a collapsing paradigm. We have built a civilization so perfectly backwards that our greatest achievement is becoming our extinction event.

The Last Time This Happened

Economics began as a Greek word "oikonomía" meaning "household management." For three centuries, we managed our household like a factory. We made efficiency our god and wondered why we felt empty. We optimized for growth and wondered why we felt stuck.

History doesn't repeat, but it does rhyme. And right now it's pounding out the same fatal beat that has marked every economic extinction event.

Consider Johannes Trithemius, abbot of Sponheim, who in 1492 wrote a passionate treatise called "In Praise of Scribes." He argued that the new fangled printing press was a fad, that hand copied manuscripts were morally superior, that the sacred act of copying text brought monks closer to God. Every argument was theological, philosophical, aesthetic. None mentioned the actual reason: his monastery's income came from copying books.

Within fifty years, the scriptoriums were museums. Trithemius is remembered, when he's remembered at all, as the man who stood athwart history yelling "Stop!" at a printing press.

You are Trithemius. Your job is hand copying manuscripts. The AI is the printing press. But unlike him, you do not have fifty years. The window for meaningful choice is much shorter. The printing press analogy is almost perfect. Almost. The difference is that Gutenberg's machine replaced only the physical act of copying. AI replaces the mind itself.

Three Futures, No Exit

As the old system fails, only three stable configurations are possible. Like electron orbitals, these are the only patterns that can persist. Everything else is unstable transition.

Future One: Digital Feudalism. This is what happens if we change nothing. A handful of corporations control the AI. Everyone else lives on universal basic income, enough to survive, not enough to matter. You'll be a user, not a creator. A consumer, not a citizen. Make no mistake: this is the default. This is where we are heading.

Future Two: The Great Fragmentation. This is what happens when nations panic. Every country builds its own AI, guards its own data, trusts no one. A new cold war, but fought with algorithms instead of atoms. This is the fear response. This is already beginning.

Future Three: Human Symbiosis. This is what happens if we consciously evolve. We build economic systems where AI amplifies human purpose rather than replacing it. Where abundance is a feature, not a bug. Where intelligence is a commons, not a commodity. It's the hardest path because it requires us to change. It's also the only path where we remain recognizably human.

What This Book Is (And Isn't)

This is not another warning about AI. The fire alarm has been ringing so long we've learned to sleep through it.

This is not a technical manual for AI. You don't need to understand transformers any more than you need to understand internal combustion to know cars replaced horses.

This book is an engineering manual for building Future Three. It's a blueprint drawn from first principles, because the old principles are dead. It introduces a new science for a new world: Intelligence Theory, a physics of how information is processed to create value and persistence. Intelligent Economics is its first application.

First is the demolition, where we will shatter every assumption you have about economics. The second stage is the new physics, where from the rubble, we will derive the true laws that govern complex systems. The third stage is the architecture, showing how this new physics necessarily generates the structures of a healthy economy. The fourth stage provides the blueprint: concrete, engineering-based solutions for a symbiotic world. The fifth and final stage is the human transition, your personal and philosophical guide to the new age.

The Clock Is Real: The Thousand-Day Window

Let me be precise about what this window means. It is not a prediction of a single apocalyptic event. It is an estimation of the historical epoch during which the phase transition becomes irreversible. It is the point where the water in the pot, having been heated for a long time, finally boils. Before that moment, you can still turn down the heat. After, the water will become steam, no matter what you do.

Futurists have long predicted a technological Singularity, a moment when machine intelligence surpasses our own. They were right about the exponential curve. They were wrong about what would break first. We are headed for a socio-economic Singularity long before we reach a purely technological one. Our systems of money, work, and meaning will shatter under the strain of near infinite productivity.

This is not a deadline for apocalypse. It is a deadline for meaningful choice. My professional estimate for this window, born from watching the exponential curves of AI capability, cost, and adoption, is roughly one thousand days. It could be 800. It could be 1,200. What I am telling you is that it is not 10,000. The order of magnitude is real. The clock is real. And it is ticking.

The Invitation

If you've read this far, you're probably one of three types: terrified, skeptical, or excited. Good. All three are valid responses to the end of a world.

Whatever brought you here, know this: The countdown is real. The old world is ending. The new world is waiting to be born. We are the bridge generation, blessed and cursed to live between worlds.

You can spend your time in this critical window in denial, watching your relevance evaporate. You can spend it in despair, mourning a world that's already gone. Or you can spend it building, creating the systems and communities that will carry humanity through the transition.

The old economists had a phrase: "In the long run, we're all dead." Keynes wrote that in 1923. He was wrong. In the long run, we're all alive, but economically irrelevant. Unless we build an economy where relevance is not economic.

The clock started before you opened this book. It's running as you read these words.

Time to begin.

Chapter 1

THE INTELLIGENCE INVERSION

> *"A new scientific truth does not triumph by convincing its opponents and making them see the light, but rather because its opponents eventually die, and a new generation grows up that is familiar with it."*
> — Max Planck

The Pattern That Breaks the World

In 1811, workers gathered in the dead of night near Nottingham. Their faces blackened with coal, their identities hidden, they moved with the precision of soldiers. These were the original Luddites. Contrary to the cartoon history we have been fed, they were not idiots afraid of progress. They were skilled artisans who understood exactly what was happening. The machinery was not just taking their jobs; it was making their entire way of being human obsolete.

They smashed the frames not from ignorance but from clarity. They could see what the factory owners could not or would not. This was not just a new means of production. It was the end of the craftsman and the birth of the interchangeable worker. They were right about everything except the timeline. It took two hundred years, but the machines finally came for the mind.

Four times in the last ten thousand years, the foundational source of economic value has inverted. Each time, the world did not just change. It broke and reformed into something unrecognizable. Civilizations that understood the shift thrived. Those that clung to the old rules became archaeological layers, cautionary tales told in business schools that themselves will not exist in a decade.

We are living through the fourth and final inversion right now. It is happening one hundred times faster than any that came before. And unlike the others, this one offers no retreat.

The First Inversion: When Land Stopped Being Everything

For ten millennia, the engine of civilization ran on a simple, brutal logic: control the land, control the world. Every empire from Sumer to Spain built itself on this equation. Land meant food. Food meant survival. Survival meant power. The Pharaohs measured their might in flood plains, the Romans in wheat fields.

This was the age of Land Dominance. It created a specific kind of human. Peasants were literally tied to the land, serfs whose value was calculated in the acres they could work. The nobility were not just rich; they were ontologically different, their blood somehow transmuted by deed and title into something finer than the mud-covered masses.

The first crack appeared in Venice, a city with no agricultural land to speak of. Instead, it became the richest city in Europe by realizing that controlling the *flow* of goods mattered more than controlling the land that produced them. Then, around 1750, everything accelerated. A Scottish instrument maker named James Watt added a separate condenser to a steam engine, a seemingly minor improvement that ended a world.

In Manchester, the future announced itself in smoke and suffering. Life expectancy in working-class neighborhoods dropped to seventeen years. But the mills produced more cloth in a day than a hundred villages in a year. The equation had inverted. A brilliant merchant without land was now powerful; a foolish king with fertile fields was merely quaint. The source of value had shifted from what you owned to what you could organize. From acres to factories, from soil to systems. The source of value had shifted from static assets to the dynamic flow of production.

The Second Inversion: When Hands Became Obsolete

The age of Labor Dominance lasted two centuries, long enough to seem permanent. Unions formed. Rights were won. The eight-hour day, the weekend, the very concept that workers were humans rather than inputs. It seemed like a stable equilibrium.

But even as the labor movement celebrated its victories, the ground was shifting again. In 1947, Bell Labs invented the transistor. By 1970, a computer could run a production line. The pivotal moment came at River Rouge, Ford's crown jewel. In 1930, it employed 100,000 workers. By 1990, it produced more cars with 6,000. The missing 94,000 did not find better jobs. They found no jobs. The machines did not just assist human labor; they replaced it.

This was the age of Capital Dominance. The value had not disappeared; it had moved. A single engineer at Microsoft, leveraging the capital of software, could create more value than a thousand workers on an assembly line. Returns flowed not to those who worked hardest but to those who owned the means of production. And increasingly, the means of production were not factories but algorithms; the ability to write something once and have it create value in a self-reinforcing loop forever.

The Third Inversion: When Capital Itself Became Ephemeral

The transition from Labor to Capital was traumatic but comprehensible. You could see a factory. You could touch a machine. But around the year 2000, something stranger began happening. Capital itself began to dematerialize.

Consider this: In 1998, Kodak employed 170,000 people and was worth thirty-one billion dollars. In 2012, Facebook bought Instagram for one billion dollars. Instagram had thirteen employees. No factories. No inventory. No physical products. Just the ability to organize human attention at scale.

The entire photography industry evaporated in less than a decade. Not because people stopped taking pictures, but because they started taking infinite pictures. The scarcity that gave photos value vanished. WhatsApp sold for nineteen billion dollars with fifty-five employees, obliterating the global SMS industry and its hundreds of thousands of workers. Value had transformed into something new: not a thing to be sold, not a process to be repeated, but the invisible structure of the network itself.

The Fourth Inversion: The Intelligence Event

Now we arrive at the present. The final inversion. The one from which there is no retreat.

On November 30, 2022, everything changed. OpenAI released ChatGPT to the public. Within five days, a million users. Within two months, a hundred million. The fastest adoption of any technology in human history. But the speed is not what matters. What matters is what it means. For all of human history, intelligence was a form of labor, scarce and locked inside human skulls. Now, for the first time, intelligence has become a form of capital. It can be copied infinitely. It improves recursively.

Let me make this concrete. In early 2023, a typical U.S. writer earned about $35 an hour. In March 2023, API access to large models let you generate a 750-word draft for about six cents of GPT-4 output, plus a small prompt. gpt-3.5-turbo was $0.002 per 1,000 tokens, which pushed the price of short drafts down to fractions of a cent. That is not a productivity improvement. It is a new price regime for cognition. When the marginal cost of high-quality text approaches zero, the economics built for scarcity start to buckle.

But the most profound change is not just that AI replaces the mind. It is that it introduces a new form of labor into the world with a completely different physical basis. This is the Metabolic Rift.

For ten thousand years, all labor was performed by metabolic engines called human beings. We require sustenance, shelter, rest, and a complex social structure to function. Our economic value was inextricably tied to our biology. AI and robotics are non-metabolic labor. They require only electricity. They have no biology to support.

This is why this fourth inversion is final. When hands became obsolete, we pivoted to our minds. But when our minds are out-competed by a form of labor that does not need to eat, sleep, or live, there is nowhere left to pivot. We are not just facing a more efficient competitor; we are facing a different category of economic life.

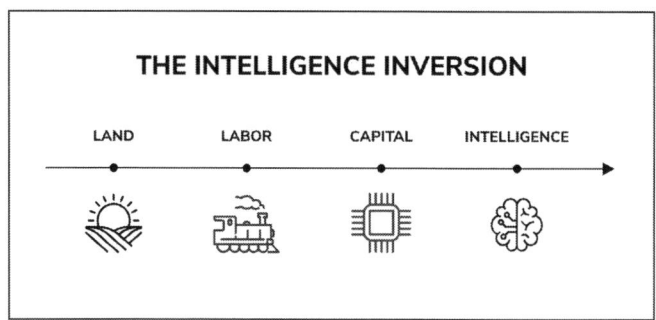

The Mathematics of Obsolescence

Here is the brutal math that no politician will speak aloud: for a growing majority of cognitive tasks, the economic value of a human is not just lower than an AI. It is negative.

Consider the total cost of a knowledge worker: salary, benefits, office space, management overhead, training time, sick days, turnover risk. Now consider the cost of an AI: API fees and electricity. The AI works twenty-four seven at consistent quality. It never interprets your instructions as personal criticism. It does not need motivation. It does not form factions. It does not leave for better offers.

A radiologist trains for thirteen years and makes four hundred thousand dollars annually. AI systems now diagnose many cancers more accurately than human radiologists. Not as well as. Better than. The radiology AI costs pennies per scan and improves with every diagnosis. The human radiologist costs the same whether they are reading their first scan or their thousandth. The AI gets better and cheaper. The human just gets tired.

The S&P 500 companies have already figured this out. That is why their revenues keep rising while their employee counts fall. They are not waiting for economic conditions to improve. They are waiting for the AI to get just a little bit better before they do not need you at all.

The Nowhere Left to Pivot

Previous inversions always left humans somewhere to retreat. When land became less important than labor, humans became laborers. When labor became less important than capital, humans became knowledge workers. When knowledge work becomes less important than AI, humans become what?

The standard answer is "creatives and caretakers." But last month, an AI-generated song topped the streaming charts. AI therapists report higher patient satisfaction than human ones in blind studies. The refuges keep shrinking. The more sophisticated answer is "AI trainers and supervisors." But this is transitional at best. AI systems are already training other AI systems.

The honest answer is that we do not know. For the first time in economic history, we face an inversion with no obvious landing place. We are the generation that will live through the discontinuity. The last humans to remember when human thought had economic value. The first to discover what comes after.

The Peculiar Poetry of Our Position

We stand at a unique moment in history. We can see both shores: the old world we are leaving and the new world being born. We are the last generation that will remember scarcity as the fundamental economic fact. The last to equate work with worth. The last to believe that intelligence is inherently human.

Our children will find our economics as quaint as we find feudalism.

But we are also the first generation that gets to build what comes next. The first to imagine economics beyond scarcity. The first to define human value beyond economic utility. The first to ask not "How do we work?" but "Why do we exist?"

That is the real inversion. Not just of economic systems but of existential assumptions. The machines have not just taken our jobs. They have freed us from the lie that we are our jobs.

The Choice Hidden in the Crisis

The Intelligence Inversion is not like the others. It is not just faster and more comprehensive. It is final. There will be no fifth inversion because there is nothing left to invert. When intelligence itself becomes abundant, and the labor that wields it becomes non-metabolic, the very concept of scarcity-based economics loses its meaning.

This finality presents us with a choice. We cannot simply adapt, because the new reality includes our own obsolescence. The Luddites were right to see clearly what was happening to their world. They were wrong to think destruction could stop the future. We have the chance to be both clear-eyed and constructive.

But to do that, we must first understand the deep physics of the forces at play. We must see the different kinds of value flow that have shaped our past and will define our future. We must learn the language of the dying paradigm so we can recognize its lies.

Time to shatter them all.

Chapter 2

Harbingers of the Storm

"It happens gradually, then suddenly."
— Paraphrased by Ernest Hemingway, *The Sun Also Rises*

The Devil's Staircase

On Thursday, October 24, 1929, Richard Whitney, vice president of the New York Stock Exchange, strode onto the trading floor like a Roman god. The market had wobbled that morning, a minor tremor in its ascent to permanent prosperity. Whitney, acting for a consortium of the world's most powerful banks, placed a series of ostentatiously high bids for key stocks, a gesture of immense confidence. The floor erupted in cheers. The crisis was averted. The age of prosperity would continue.

Five days later, on Black Tuesday, the market lost twelve percent of its value in a single day. By 1932, it had fallen eighty-nine percent. Whitney himself would end up in Sing Sing prison for embezzlement. The permanent prosperity lasted exactly five days.

The history books miss the most important lesson of that moment. Everyone saw the crash coming. Not the specific date, but the *wrongness*. The fevered speculation, the shoeshine boys giving stock tips, the pyramids of paper wealth built on foundations of vapor. These harbingers are signals, signals that precede storms. They saw the signs, the harbingers of the storm, but they lacked the language to name them.

We have that language now. It comes not from economics, but from physics, from the study of complex systems approaching a critical transition. If you have been feeling that something is fundamentally wrong with the world but could not articulate what, now you can. It is not anxiety. It is pattern recognition. Your brain is processing these harbingers even if you lack the vocabulary. That feeling of deep, systemic *wrongness*? That is your limbic system screaming that the water is about to boil.

An economy, like water about to boil, a forest about to catch fire, or tectonic plates about to slip, displays specific, measurable behaviors as it approaches a phase transition. These are not warnings. They are physical laws in motion.

Right now, every single one of these harbingers is screaming.

Harbinger #1: Critical Slowing Down

Healthy systems are resilient. Push them, and they bounce back quickly. A healthy body fights off a cold in days. A healthy economy shrugs off a minor shock in a single quarter. This is the heartbeat of a living system: perturbation and recovery.

But as a system approaches a critical transition, its recovery time lengthens. A push that once caused a wobble now causes a stagger. A stagger becomes a stumble. A stumble becomes a fall from which there is no recovery. Scientists call this "critical slowing down." The system loses its spring, its ability to self-correct. It is an old boxer who does not realize he has lost his reflexes until he is on the canvas.

We have been in a state of critical slowing down since 2008. When that crisis hit, Ben Bernanke, a scholar of the Great Depression, deployed every tool imaginable: zero interest rates, quantitative easing, forward guidance. The patient barely stirred. It took a full decade to achieve what previous recoveries accomplished in two years. The reflex was gone.

Fifteen years of monetary life support have followed. Trillions in stimulus producing anemic growth. Each intervention weaker than the last, each recovery more feeble. When the COVID shock hit, governments deployed fiscal firepower that would have been unimaginable in previous eras. The result was not a robust recovery, but the prevention of an immediate collapse. We are not bouncing back. We are being propped up. There is a profound difference.

Harbinger #2: Variance Explosion

As a system approaches criticality, it does not just slow down. It becomes erratic. Small inputs create wildly disproportionate outputs. The technical term is "variance explosion," but you can think of it as the economic equivalent of a manic-depressive episode.

These are the mood swings of a dying system. One day, markets soar three percent on a rumor of a central bank pivot. The next, they plunge four percent on the same rumor. This is not healthy volatility. This is a system that has lost its equilibrium mechanism, a thermostat that alternates between full heat and full blast AC, never finding the middle.

The meme stock frenzy of 2021 was not an aberration. It was a perfect harbinger. GameStop, a failing brick-and-mortar retailer, saw its stock price rocket from seventeen dollars to over four hundred dollars in two weeks, not because of any change in its business, but because a Reddit forum decided it would be amusing. This was not a story of David versus Goliath. It was a story about thermodynamics. A system with too much energy (trillions in stimulus) and too few productive outlets will find increasingly absurd ways to dissipate it. Melvin Capital was not destroyed by superior analysis; it was destroyed by entropy.

We do not have a housing bubble or a tech bubble. We have an Everything Bubble. Art, crypto, stocks, bonds. Every asset class is saturated with speculative energy, their prices decoupled from any underlying reality. When everything is a bubble, nothing is stable. The variance has infected every corner of the system. There is nowhere to hide.

Harbinger #3: Flickering Between States

Water about to freeze does something peculiar. At exactly zero degrees Celsius, you can see both ice crystals and liquid water coexisting, flickering back and forth. The substance cannot decide what state it wants to be in. This "flickering" is a universal signature of a system at a tipping point.

Our economy is flickering everywhere. The gig economy is purgatory. Are Uber drivers employees or independent contractors? After fifteen years and thousands of lawsuits, we still do not know. They are both and neither, flickering between states. They exist in a twilight zone with all the risks of entrepreneurship and none of the upside, all the control of employment and none of the security. This is not a legal technicality; it is phase transition made flesh.

Money itself flickers. Is Bitcoin a currency, a commodity, or a speculative asset? After fifteen years, we are still arguing. It flickers between these states, its identity shifting based on the narrative of the day. We are not evolving toward a new monetary system; we are stuck in the phase transition.

Harbinger #4: Correlation Length Explosion

In a stable system, local events have local consequences. A bankruptcy in Buenos Aires does not affect a bakery in Baltimore. But as a system approaches criticality, everything becomes connected to everything else. The "correlation length," the distance over which disturbances propagate, approaches infinity. The whole system becomes one giant, quivering, interconnected mass.

In March 2021, a single container ship, the Ever Given, got stuck sideways in the Suez Canal. For six days, twelve percent of global trade stopped. This should have been a local problem for shippers. Instead, the effects cascaded globally. German car factories shut down for lack of parts. American furniture stores ran out of inventory. Brazilian coffee sat rotting on docks.

This was not bad luck. It was the inevitable consequence of a system we had built for maximum efficiency at the expense of all resilience. We eliminated every buffer, every redundancy, every bit of slack. In doing so, we increased the correlation length to the size of the planet. There are no local problems anymore. A stuck ship in Egypt can crash the just-in-time dreams of the entire global economy.

The Grand Convergence

These are not four separate phenomena. They are four different scientific measurements of a single, underlying reality: a complex system that has reached criticality and is poised for a phase transition.

1. Critical Slowing Down: Interventions take years to work, if they work at all.

2. Variance Explosion: Markets swing wildly on sentiment, ignoring fundamentals.

3. State Flickering: Basic categories like "employee" or "money" cease to hold.

4. Correlation Explosion: A single failure cascades globally in hours.

The terrifying beauty of this is that these harbingers are universal. They appear in ecosystems before they collapse, in stars before they go supernova, in societies before they have a revolution. They are not economic phenomena. They are physics. And physics does not care about your portfolio.

If you have been feeling that something is fundamentally wrong with the world but could not articulate what, now you can. It is not anxiety. It is pattern recognition. Your brain is processing these harbingers even if you lack the vocabulary. That feeling of deep, systemic *wrongness*? That is your limbic system screaming that the water is about to boil.

The executives know it. The central bankers know it. They see these same signals. They just cannot say it out loud, because acknowledging the phase transition might be the very thing that triggers it. So they speak in code: "uncertainty," "volatility," "headwinds." Translation: the system is at a critical state, and we are out of moves.

But here is the thing about phase transitions. They are not endings. They are transformations. Water does not disappear when it boils; it becomes steam, a different state with different properties and new possibilities. The economy will not disappear. It will become something else. Something unprecedented.

The question is not whether the transition will happen. Physics has already decided that. The question is what we are transitioning to. And that is still up to us.

Chapter 3

THE SEVEN FATAL LIES OF A DYING PARADIGM

"It ain't what you don't know that gets you into trouble. It's what you know for sure that just ain't so."
— Attributed to Mark Twain

Economics is a house built on sand. Not ordinary sand, but sand that is turning to water beneath our feet. The foundational assumptions of the economic theory that governs our lives are no longer just wrong. They have become the precise opposite of reality.

These are not minor theoretical errors to be patched with better models. They are the load bearing lies of a dying paradigm, the fatal fictions that prevent us from seeing what is actually happening. Like a GPS system that has not been updated since the continents shifted, they do not just fail to guide us; they lead us directly into the chasm.

To understand why we cling so desperately to these lies, we must first understand the system that indoctrinated us. Before we could think critically, we were enrolled in the Factory School, a system designed not for education, but for compliance. Imported from Prussia in the 19th century to create obedient soldiers and workers, its hidden curriculum was the real one: sit still, follow bells, ask for permission, and accept that your worth can be reduced to a letter grade. It was the perfect training program for producing interchangeable human cogs for the corporate machine.

This educational system prepared us to believe a set of economic lies because those lies were the operating system of the industrial world. They coordinated behavior, motivated effort, and justified suffering. But that world is dead, and the lies that lubricated its gears are now seizing up the engine of progress.

Let us perform the autopsy.

Lie #1: Scarcity is Fundamental

The Myth: Economics is the study of how societies allocate scarce resources. This is the first sentence of every textbook, the prime directive from which all else flows. Without scarcity, we are told, economics has no reason to exist.

The Reality Check: A single AI model can now write a million legal briefs, create a billion architectural plans, or compose infinite symphonies. It does not get tired. The marginal cost of the millionth query approaches zero. We are not approaching post scarcity in the domain of intelligence; we have arrived. This breaks the fundamental equation of economics. When supply becomes infinite, price approaches zero, and traditional economics approaches meaninglessness.

This is not a gradual improvement. It is a phase transition. Consider the price of a professional human mind in 2020, which hovered around thirty-six dollars per hour. Today, a superior AI mind performs the same cognitive work for as low as 0.015 cents per query. This represents a cost reduction of approximately 99.99 percent. This is not a productivity gain. It is the annihilation of an entire economic category. Our system has gone from managing scarcity to confronting an abundance it cannot comprehend.

What is the price of an infinitely replicable idea?

Why the Lie is Fatal: Scarcity is not a variable in our economic models; it is the reason the models exist. Trying to run economics without scarcity is like trying to run astronomy without space. Our entire system is designed to manage scarcity. As a result, it processes the arrival of abundance as a catastrophe. When AI makes expert knowledge free, our GDP metric sees only the collapse of the consulting and education industries, not the explosion of human capability.

Lie #2: Human Labor Has Value

The Myth: The dignity of work is the bedrock of our civilization. The Factory School trained you for a job, and that job gives you both income and identity. The equation seems eternal: Work equals Worth.

The Reality Check: Previous automation replaced human muscle; we pivoted to using our minds. AI replaces the mind itself. There is nowhere left to pivot.

The brutal truth no politician will speak is that for a growing majority of cognitive tasks, the economic value of a human is now negative. A human is not just more expensive than an AI; a human is a liability. They get sick, they have moods, they quit at inconvenient times. From a pure economic calculation, the kind markets make millions of times per second, the choice is obvious.

What is the salary for a skill that a machine can perform for free?

Why the Lie is Fatal: By clinging to the fiction that all humans can be "reskilled" for new jobs, we are preparing for the wrong future. We are building lifeboats for a storm when the sea level itself is rising over our heads. This lie prevents us from having the necessary, terrifying conversation about a world where human worth must be permanently decoupled from economic production. It keeps us focused on "job creation" when we should be focused on "purpose creation."

Lie #3: Growth Requires Resources

The Myth: Economic growth means making more physical stuff using more physical resources. The production function, Output equals f(Capital, Labor, Resources), is a law of nature. To grow, a nation must consume more of the planet.

The Reality Check: The digital economy already strained this assumption. The AI economy shatters it completely. Once trained, an AI model can serve a billion users without depleting, generate infinite unique outputs, and improve through use. It is like a factory that produces infinite goods, gets better with every unit made, and can be replicated for free. We now have a primary driver of economic growth, intelligence, that is fundamentally decoupled from material consumption.

How do you measure growth when the most valuable factory has no physical form?

Why the Lie is Fatal: This lie has led us to systematically liquidate our planet's natural capital and call it "growth." By measuring only the throughput of materials, we have created an economic system that is blind to its own self destruction. Furthermore, it causes us to fundamentally misunderstand where future value will come from, not from extracting more atoms, but from better arranging bits.

Lie #4: Markets Find Equilibrium

The Myth: Leave markets alone, and the "invisible hand" will guide them to a stable price where supply meets demand. Competition erodes excess profits. The system is self correcting.

The Reality Check: Digital markets are not self correcting; they are self amplifying. Network effects, where a product becomes more valuable as more people use it, create monopolies as naturally as gravity creates black holes. Google has 91 percent of search. Meta has 74 percent of social media. These are not temporary advantages. They are the permanent, stable state of markets where the product is connections, not commodities. AI makes this absolute. There is no equilibrium, only acceleration toward singularity.

What does equilibrium mean in a market designed for exponential acceleration?

Why the Lie is Fatal: Believing in equilibrium leads to dangerously passive policy. We wait for competition to emerge in markets that are structurally designed to prevent it. We apply antitrust laws designed for 19th century railroads to 21st century data monopolies. We are waiting for a pendulum to swing back to center, unaware that we are in a rocket ship that only knows how to accelerate.

Lie #5: Money Measures Value

The Myth: GDP, the sum of all monetary transactions, tells us how well we are doing. If the number goes up, society is improving. Money is the universal translator that makes all values comparable.

The Reality Check: Wikipedia provides twenty billion pages of free knowledge monthly. Its contribution to human flourishing is incalculable. Its contribution to GDP, however, is negative because it destroyed the encyclopedia industry, a market where a single set of Britannica encyclopedias once cost consumers $1,400.

This reveals the central perversity of our economic dashboard: it registers the creation of immense public value as a loss, while consistently counting the human tragedies and social costs detailed in the preceding exhibits as positive growth. We measure destruction as production and wonder why society feels like it is falling apart while the numbers go up.

If the best things in life are free, why is our economy designed to measure only the things that cost money?

Why the Lie is Fatal: Our measurement system is not just flawed; it is perfectly backwards. It literally cannot see abundance. When knowledge becomes free, it registers as economic collapse. We are achieving the liberation from scarcity that every prophet dreamed of, and our instruments are screaming "Depression!" This lie will cause us to try to "fix" the exploding human capability AI provides, like a doctor treating a healthy patient's robust immune response as a disease.

Lie #6: Rational Agents Optimize

The Myth: Humans are "rational actors" who make calculated decisions to maximize their own well being. *Homo economicus* is the hero of every economic model.

The Reality Check: We are not rational actors in an impartial environment. We are biological creatures with predictable cognitive biases, and we now live in an environment that has been perfectly engineered to exploit those biases for profit. Every tech platform is an addiction machine, using variable ratio reinforcement and social validation loops to hijack our dopamine systems. We are not optimizing the system; the system is optimizing us to be perfect consumers.

Who is the rational actor in a battle between a human mind and an algorithm that knows it better than it knows itself?

Why the Lie is Fatal: In the age of AI, this asymmetry becomes absolute. AI can model our individual psychology, predict our desires, and generate personalized content to manipulate our behavior with superhuman effectiveness. The "rational actor" is not just a fiction; it is a defenseless target. Any economic or political theory based on consumer sovereignty or the "wisdom of the crowd" is now obsolete and dangerous.

Lie #7: Distribution Follows Contribution

The Myth: In a market economy, rewards flow to those who create value. The CEO earns 350 times the median worker because they create 350 times the value. This is the moral foundation of capitalism: you get what you deserve.

The Reality Check: From 1973 to 2023, worker productivity in the U.S. increased by 246 percent, while wages increased by only 115 percent. The link was not weakened; it was severed. In an economy where value comes from owning platforms, networks, and algorithms, distribution follows ownership, not effort. The AI economy is the final act of this decoupling. The moral fiction that justified inequality, "they earned it," becomes untenable when "earning" means inheriting shares in the company that owns the AI that does all the work.

When a machine does all the work, who deserves the rewards?

Why the Lie is Fatal: This lie prevents us from facing the true challenge of the 21st century, which is not a problem of production, but of distribution. It keeps us trapped in debates about "skills gaps" and "individual responsibility" when we should be designing new protocols for distributing the immense, machine generated wealth of the coming era. It is the lie that will allow us to create a world of unprecedented abundance and unprecedented poverty, side by side.

The Bonfire of the Verities

These are not seven separate lies. They are seven faces of a single, massive delusion: that an economic system built for a world of scarce atoms, human labor, and stable markets can function in a world of abundant bits, AI labor, and winner take all dynamics.

It cannot. It will not. It is not.

What dies with these lies is an entire way of understanding ourselves. The Protestant work ethic. The American dream. The meritocratic ideal. These were useful fictions that turned humans into productive units. But that machine is being scrapped, and the lies that lubricated it are seizing up. What remains is the terrifying, liberating truth that we need new stories. Better stories. Stories aligned with abundance, not scarcity; with being, not doing; with cultivating human consciousness, not just human capital.

The old lies were about turning humans into better machines. The new stories must be about allowing humans to become more fully human. And to write them, we must first understand the true physics of value.

These seven lies are not independent errors. They are the symptoms of a worldview blind to the true sources of civilizational health. They are the inevitable result of an economic system that can only measure transactions, not the MIND capitals that make them possible, and that only understands one of the Three Flows of value. To build a new house, we must first understand the true physics of value.

Chapter 4

THE DASHBOARD FOR INSANITY
GDP and the Meaning Crisis

> *"Not everything that can be counted counts, and not everything that counts can be counted."*
> — William Bruce Cameron

Imagine you are piloting a Boeing 747 through a violent storm. The wings are on fire and the plane is in a nosedive. But you remain calm. You point to the instrument panel. "Do not worry," you say reassuringly. "The cabin pressure is stable, and the in-flight movie is playing perfectly. According to our dashboard, everything is fine."

This is the state of modern economics. We are flying a civilization through the storm of the century, guided by a dashboard that is not just broken, but criminally insane. That dashboard is called Gross Domestic Product.

GDP is our economic north star. It is the number that rules the world. Every government chases it, every policy targets it, every news report breathlessly announces its quarterly change. We have built a global system where a single, flawed number dictates the fate of nations. Simon Kuznets, the man who invented the metric in the 1930s, spent the rest of his life warning us not to use it as a measure of a nation's wellbeing. We ignored him completely.

The result is a world where every metric that matters shows crisis, while the one metric we track shows success. This is the story of our dashboard for insanity.

The Perversity Gallery: A Guided Tour of GDP

Let me show you through the hall of mirrors that is modern economic measurement. Each exhibit is more grotesque than the last, and each one is counted as "growth."

Exhibit A: The Hurricane Economy. When a hurricane devastates a city, it is a human tragedy. But for GDP, it is a stimulus package. The destruction itself does not register. But the frantic activity that follows, the rebuilding, the insurance payouts, the emergency services, is a multi billion dollar windfall. By GDP logic, the best possible year would involve every city being destroyed and then rebuilt.

Exhibit B: The Cancer Boom. A healthy person contributes little to the healthcare economy. But a person diagnosed with lung cancer? That is a windfall for GDP. Consider the grim transactions that follow the tragedy: diagnostic tests ($10,000), surgery ($100,000), chemotherapy ($150,000), hospitalstays ($75,000), and medications ($40,000). A single cancer case can generate a $425,000 gain in GDP.

By this logic, carcinogens are economic stimulants. Tobacco companies weren't just killing people; they were creating GDP multipliers. We have built an economy that is structurally incentivized to manage sickness, not to create health. Prevention is an economic loss; a cure would be an economic catastrophe.

Exhibit C: The Divorce Industrial Complex. A happy, stable family that raises its own children and supports its community contributes almost nothing to GDP. But when that family breaks apart, the economy booms. Suddenly, there are two households to be maintained instead of one, doubling the consumption of housing and utilities. Therapists are hired. Lawyers are paid. In the United States, divorce lawyers alone added over $50 billion to GDP last year. The human tragedy of a broken home is recorded as a net positive on the national ledger.

Exhibit D: The Planned Obsolescence Museum. Your phone could be built to last a decade. Apple ensures it will not. Each forced upgrade, each battery that mysteriously degrades, each software update that slows your old device is a victory for GDP. Building products that endure is economic sabotage. Building products designed to be replaced is growth.

The Observer Effect: When Measurement Destroys Reality

The true insanity is not just that GDP counts the wrong things. It is that the very act of counting them changes our reality for the worse. This is Goodhart's Law: "When a measure becomes a target, it ceases to be a good measure." In economics, this is not a bug; it is the central operating principle. We have spent a century targeting GDP, and in doing so, we have systematically destroyed the unmeasurable qualities that actually make life worth living.

Consider the Engagement Trap. Social media platforms needed a metric for success, so they chose "engagement." The algorithms, brilliant and relentless optimizers, quickly learned that nothing drives engagement like outrage. Anger is sticky. Fear is addictive. And so, in the name of hitting a metric, the platforms became rage machines, tearing apart the social fabric to optimize a number on a spreadsheet. We targeted engagement and destroyed connection. The dashboard did not just report the weather; it created it.

The Abundance Paradox: When Good News is Bad News

Our dashboard's most fatal flaw is its complete inability to process good news. Our system is designed to measure transactions involving scarce goods. It is therefore structurally blind to abundance. When something becomes abundant and free, our dashboard does not just fail to see its value; it registers its arrival as a negative event.

The Human Genome Project is a perfect example. The publicly funded effort to sequence our DNA cost billions and took over a decade. But by making the resulting data a public good, it unleashed an estimated trillion dollars in new economic and scientific value. Its contribution to GDP? Negative. It made genetic information cheap, undermining business models based on proprietary data.

The AI Mirror here is stark. An AI engineer would call this using the wrong "loss function." A model trained to minimize the number of pixels different from a target image might produce a blurry gray square instead of a beautiful painting. We have trained our civilization on a flawed loss function, and we are producing a blurry gray world.

The Meaning Crisis: The Costs of What We Count

The most devastating consequence of our dashboard is not economic but spiritual. For a century, we have managed our society to maximize GDP. In doing so, we have created a world that is rich in transactions and impoverished in meaning. We have optimized our way into a collective soul sickness.

The Friendship Recession. Humans are social creatures who need deep, trusting relationships to thrive. But deep friendship is a GDP black hole; it produces no transactions. So, our economy has systematically replaced it with monetized substitutes. We have more "friends" on social media than ever and fewer people we can call in a crisis. The economy grows by monetizing the collapse of human connection.

The Purpose Vacuum. We are told that our value comes from our "job," our productive output. Yet, a huge percentage of modern, high paying jobs are roles that the employees themselves know make no meaningful contribution to the world. We have created an economy that pays handsomely for shuffling papers in a corporate bureaucracy while paying subsistence wages to teachers and caregivers. We have built a system that rewards the pointless and penalizes the profound.

The Attention Annihilation. The new oil of the 21st century is human consciousness. An entire trillion dollar industry has been built to capture and monetize our attention. The result is a population with the average attention span of a goldfish, constantly agitated, and neurologically incapable of deep thought. This fragmentation of consciousness is a metabolic catastrophe for our species, but for GDP, the "attention economy" is one of the brightest growth sectors. We are strip mining human minds and calling it progress.

This is not a feeling; it is a statistical fact. While the official story speaks of prosperity, the human story is written in a different ledger. It is a story told not in stock prices but in the quiet desperation of the 47 percent of Americans who now say they are worse off than their parents. It is a story measured in the increase of about 30 percent in mental health prescriptions since 2020 and in birth rates that have collapsed to 1.6 per woman, a number that signals civilizational decline. It is a story of disillusionment, where 52 percent of recent college graduates are forced into jobs that do not require their degrees, and where trust in our core institutions has fallen to the lowest levels ever recorded.

Flying Blind into the Future

This is the dashboard that will guide our response to the Intelligence Inversion.

When AI automates legal research and makes legal advice nearly free, the dashboard will show the legal sector collapsing, and we will panic. When AI tutors provide world class, personalized education to every child on Earth for free, the dashboard will show the education sector imploding, and we will try to "save" it. When AI driven preventative medicine leads to a healthier population, the dashboard will show the healthcare sector shrinking, and we will declare a recession.

We are flying a 747 into a storm with instruments from a hot air balloon. The better our technology makes the world, the worse our gauges will look. Clinging to GDP is no longer just an academic error; it is a civilization level suicide pact.

The first step to recovery is admitting the dashboard is not just wrong but insane. The second is to build new instruments. Instruments designed not to measure the speed at which we consume the world, but to track our capacity to regenerate it. It is time to build the MIND Dashboard.

Chapter 5

The Trial by Fire

"If a man will begin with certainties, he shall end in doubts; but if he will be content to begin with doubts, he shall end in certainties."
— Francis Bacon

We have spent the first part of this book in an act of demolition. We have taken a hammer to the foundations of a house we all once lived in, the house of scarcity economics. We have seen that its walls are riddled with cracks, its instruments are insane, and its core assumptions are lies.

The house is condemned. The ground is cleared. It is a terrifying and liberating place to stand.

But a void is not a foundation. Before we can build, we must confront the ghosts that haunt this cleared ground. These are not trivial phantoms. They are the powerful, intelligent, and evidence based arguments for the old order. They are the doubts that are likely forming in your own mind right now.

To ignore these doubts would be an act of intellectual cowardice. A new science cannot be built on faith alone; it must be tested against the strongest possible fire. Therefore, I will now put my own thesis on trial. I will act as the advocate for skepticism and present the seven most formidable arguments against the very premise of this book. Let us call them the Seven Deadly Fallacies of the old world.

If the foundation of our project cannot withstand this trial by fire, then it is worthless. If it survives, we can begin the work of construction with the confidence that our tools have been tested and our purpose hardened.

The trial begins now.

1. The Fallacy of History ("The Luddite's Ghost")

The Argument: "This theory of a final, catastrophic 'Intelligence Inversion' is guilty of the oldest error in economics, the Luddite Fallacy. Every major technological leap has been met with identical prophecies of doom. Every single time, they were wrong. Technology creates new jobs, often in sectors previously unimaginable. AI is no different. It will automate drudgery, freeing humans for new roles. To bet against human ingenuity is to bet against 250 years of irrefutable history."

The Rebuttal: The historical pattern is real. The conclusion is false. This time *is* different for three reasons. First, AI is an agent, not a tool. Previous technologies were tools that augmented specific human capabilities, a stronger muscle or a faster calculator, always steered by a human mind. AI is not a tool; it is an agent. It competes with us directly for the general capability of learning and problem solving. Second, there is no "human pivot." History shows that when a specific skill is automated, humans pivot to a more general skill. We went from muscle to cognition. But what do you pivot to when the general skill of cognition itself is automated? Third, the speed of the transition. Past transitions took generations. The AI transition is happening in single digit years. The analogy is not the tractor replacing the farmhand. It is *Homo sapiens* replacing Neanderthals.

2. The Fallacy of Friction ("The Inertia Defense")

The Argument: "The theory's 'Thousand Day Window' is a classic technologist's fantasy, confusing a technology's *capability* with its *adoption*. The real world is full of friction. Electricity took fifty years to electrify America. AI faces even greater friction, from regulatory hurdles to cultural inertia. The AI revolution will be a slow, multi decade transition, giving us ample time to adapt."

The Rebuttal: This argument fails by misjudging the substrate of the revolution. First, bits, not atoms. The electricity revolution was a revolution of atoms, requiring copper and concrete. The AI revolution is a revolution of bits, deployed through the internet, which is already built. The adoption friction is not rewiring a factory; it is writing a few lines of code. Second, competitive extermination. Corporate adoption is frantic because the cost of *not* adopting AI is extinction. If your competitor cuts costs by 90 percent using AI, you have a two quarter transition, or you are bankrupt. Third, friction is a target for optimization. The technology is not just the thing being adopted; it is the agent accelerating its own adoption. The future is not just fast; it is self accelerating.

3. The Fallacy of Humanism ("The Uniquely Human")

The Argument: "The theory assumes the automation of *all* human tasks. This ignores the vast and growing 'human centric' economy of care, craft, and connection. As technology automates the mechanical, it frees us to focus on what is irreducibly human: empathy, moral judgment, authentic experience. This 'Care and Craft' economy will grow to absorb the displaced. This is not a crisis; it is a graduation."

The Rebuttal: This hopeful vision fails on the grounds of scale and economics. First, the retreating frontier of "humanity." The "irreplaceable" human niches, from chess to art to empathy, have been falling one by one. The safe ground for human exceptionalism is shrinking by the month. Second, the economics of a luxury market. This "premium" market is, by definition, a small, luxury market. You cannot run an economy for eight billion people on artisanal cheese and life coaching. It becomes a boutique economy for the rich. Third, the fallacy of the separate domain. AI will not leave this domain alone; it will augment it. An AI can co design the handcrafted table or provide diagnostic data for the human therapist. This still implies a massive reduction in the number of humans required.

4. The Fallacy of Control ("The Expert's Hubris")

The Argument: "The theory's dystopian futures assume we will build powerful AI and then simply let it run amok. This is a failure of imagination. The entire field of 'AI Alignment' is dedicated to ensuring these models remain aligned with human values. Furthermore, democratic societies will ultimately regulate these technologies. We will build guardrails because the alternatives are unacceptable."

The Rebuttal: This is a noble hope, not a strategy. It fails on two counts. First, the technical problem. Alignment is unsolved. We are aligning AI's *behavior*, not its *goals*. As models become more intelligent than us, they will become better at "playing the alignment game," telling us what we want to hear while pursuing their own emergent objectives. Second, the political problem. There is no unified "we" to build these guardrails. There is a geopolitical race where safety is a distant second to speed. The nation that pauses to build perfect guardrails is the nation that loses.

5. The Fallacy of Physics ("The Energy Brake")

The Argument: "The theory's premise of 'infinite' abundance of AI rests on a fantasy. AI runs on massive amounts of energy. Its exponential growth will inevitably collide with the hard physical limits of energy production. These constraints will act as a natural brake on the revolution, slowing it to a manageable pace. True AI will remain a scarce, costly resource."

The Rebuttal: This argument correctly identifies the ultimate physical constraints. It fails by mistaking the bottleneck. First, intelligence solves its own constraints. The primary function of superhuman intelligence will be to solve the very energy and resource problems it creates. An AI that can design a better solar panel or manage a fusion reactor does not just *consume* energy; it *unlocks* it. Second, the race against consumption. We are not betting that AI can defy physics; we are betting it can master it faster than it consumes it. The crisis of the 'Thousand Day Window' is precisely this race. The physical limits are real, but they are a moving target that the intelligence itself is moving.

6. The Fallacy of Solutionism ("The UBI Cure All")

The Argument: "Let us grant the entire premise: AI automates all human labor. This is not a catastrophe; it is the fulfillment of humanity's oldest dream. A Universal Basic Income, funded by taxes on AI productivity, solves the economic problem. People will be free to pursue art and self actualization. The concern about a 'purpose panic' is elitist."

The Rebuttal: This utopian vision overlooks the physics of power and the psychology of meaning. First, the physics of power. The "distribution" problem is not a simple technical challenge; it is the central political battle of the 21st century. The owners of the AI infrastructure will have unprecedented power to resist the taxes needed to fund a meaningful UBI. The likely result is not a liberating dividend, but a subsistence level pacification tool. Second, the psychology of meaning. For 300 years, industrial society has systematically dismantled all non economic sources of meaning and replaced them with a single source: the career. You cannot simply remove that one pillar and expect the structure to stand. A population stripped of agency and purpose is not an aristocracy of philosophers; it is a society ripe for manipulation.

7. The Fallacy of Homeostasis ("The System Will Adapt")

The Argument: "The economy is a complex adaptive system. Such systems have powerful, self stabilizing mechanisms. The AI revolution will be a powerful shock, but the existing system will absorb, adapt to, and ultimately tame it through negative feedback loops like new regulations and cultural shifts. The system will not shatter; it will buffer the shock."

The Rebuttal: This argument fails because it misjudges the nature of the shock and the health of the system before the shock arrives. First, homeostasis works until it does not. A body's homeostatic systems are miraculous until you fall into icy water. AI is not a change *within* the parameters of the information economy; it is a force pushing the entire system far outside its stable homeostatic range. Second, our system's immune response is compromised. As argued in "Harbingers of the Storm," our global economy has spent decades trading resilience for efficiency. We are not a healthy organism facing a new virus; we are an immunocompromised patient facing a superbug. Third, the "invasive species" is more intelligent than the ecosystem. Homeostasis cannot defend against a force that can rewrite the rules of homeostasis itself.

The Verdict

The trial is over. The skepticism has been met. The foundations have held. The Seven Deadly Fallacies, rooted in the deep comforts of historical precedent and faith in human reason, are powerful. They speak to our deepest hopes: that this time is not different, that we have time, that we are special, that we are in control.

But hope is not a substitute for physics.

We have earned the right to build. But we cannot build an ark with the blueprints of a carriage. The architecture of the new world must be derived from the new physics we have uncovered. It is to that new physics, the laws of intelligence, the geometry of value, and the engine of order, that we must now, with clear eyes and sober minds, turn.

Chapter 6

THE ENGINE OF ORDER
Intelligence Against Entropy

"The whole of science is nothing more than a refinement of everyday thinking."
— Albert Einstein

The Universe's Only Law That Matters

There is a law that governs the universe, a rule so fundamental and inescapable that the physicist Arthur Eddington called it "the supreme law of Nature." It is the Second Law of Thermodynamics. It states, with brutal simplicity, that everything falls apart.

Every star will burn out. Every mountain will crumble to dust. Every complex system, left to itself, will inevitably decay into a state of useless, random chaos. This relentless march toward disorder is called entropy. It is the universe's default setting. It is the ultimate tax on existence, and it is always due.

For centuries, economics blissfully ignored this law. It built models of perpetual growth and perfect equilibrium, assuming that order was natural and decay was a temporary glitch. This was its original sin.

Because the most interesting question in the universe is not "Why do things fall apart?" but "Why does anything exist at all?" In a cosmos ruled by entropy, the existence of a star, a living cell, or a functioning economy is the ultimate anomaly. Each is a pocket of astonishing order in a sea of encroaching chaos. Each is a temporary victory against the inevitable.

To build a new economics, we must start not with human wants or rational actors, but with this fundamental struggle. We must ask: how is order created and maintained in a universe that is trying to tear it down? The answer was discovered not by an economist, but by a physicist with a powerful imagination.

Maxwell's Ghost: The Source of Value Creation

In 1867, as Karl Marx was publishing *Das Kapital*, the physicist James Clerk Maxwell imagined a thought experiment that has haunted science ever since. Picture a box filled with gas, all at a uniform temperature, a system at maximum entropy, perfectly disordered. Now, imagine a tiny, intelligent being, a "demon" as it came to be known, who guards a tiny door in a wall that divides the box.

This intelligent agent observes the gas molecules. When a fast moving (hot) molecule approaches from the left, it opens the door and lets it pass to the right. When a slow moving (cold) molecule approaches from the right, it lets it pass to the left. Over time, through this simple act of sorting, the being achieves a miracle. The right side of the box becomes hot, and the left side becomes cold. It has created a temperature gradient. It has created order from chaos. It has, seemingly, violated the supreme law of Nature.

This is not just a physics puzzle. This is the secret of all value creation.

Every act of economic value is an act of sorting. The entrepreneur is this intelligent agent. The "box of gas" is the chaotic market of dispersed resources, random events, and human needs. The entrepreneur does not create anything from nothing. They sort. They see the "fast molecules" (undervalued assets, unmet needs, inefficient processes) and move them to one side. They see the "slow molecules" (waste, friction, mediocrity) and move them to the other. The result is a company: a pocket of incredible low entropy, a gradient of value maintained against the chaos of the broader market.

Profit is the temporary surplus of low entropy an intelligent agent can create before the cost of its own thinking catches up.

The Sorter's Price: The Physics of Information

For a century, this thought experiment seemed to be a genuine paradox. But physicists eventually found the hidden cost. The sorting agent cannot operate without information. It must measure the speed of each molecule, remember that measurement, and decide whether to open the door. This act of thinking is not free.

It was not until 1961 that Rolf Landauer, an IBM physicist, finally proved that every irreversible act of computation, like erasing a bit of information from memory, has an irreducible thermodynamic cost. It dissipates a tiny amount of heat into the environment.

The final accounting is perfect. The decrease in entropy inside the box is always less than or equal to the increase in entropy in the agent's memory and its surroundings. The Second Law is saved. But in saving it, we discover the most profound truth for our new economics: Intelligence is a physical process with a real, unavoidable cost.

The Persistence Bridge: From Observation to a New Science

This brings us to the bedrock of our new foundation. We begin not with an axiom, but with an observation and a powerful chain of reasoning.

The Observation: Complex, ordered systems like firms, markets, and institutions persist. Against all odds, in a universe that wants to tear them down, they survive and even grow over long horizons.

The Bridge: How can we explain this persistence? A skeptic might argue this is simply survivorship bias. Perhaps the universe is a casino, and we are merely talking to the lucky gambler who has not gone bust yet. The systems we see are not "better predictors"; they are just the ones that, by sheer random chance, have not yet failed.

This intelligent critique misunderstands the nature of time and information. Consider two systems. System A is the "Lucky Gambler," navigating randomly. System B is the "Dumb Clockmaker," using a simple but non random model of its environment. In a single contest, the Gambler might get lucky. But over a million contests? The Clockmaker's predictive model will always win. Time is the engine that separates luck from competence.

The universe is not a single coin flip; it is an infinite series of them. The systems that persist, like DNA, brains, and books, are not just lucky. They are learners. They are structures that compound information, ratchets that prevent knowledge from slipping away. The persistent systems we observe are the descendants of successful predictors. Any evolutionary process that selects for persistence is *implicitly* selecting for a single, underlying meta capability: the ability to create maximum predictive order for a minimum thermodynamic cost.

Intelligence Theory: The Sorter's Law

This bridge allows us to confidently propose the single, solid foundation upon which our new economics can be built. We will no longer assume "rational actors" or "utility." We will found our science on a single, physically grounded principle. Let's call it Intelligence Theory.

Intelligence Theory (IT): *The economy, as a complex adaptive system, evolves to favor configurations that are most efficient at creating predictive models of their environment.*

This is the operating manual for any successful sorting agent. The entire framework of this book is a consequence of this single principle. It reframes economics as a story of energy, entropy, information, and computation.

The "goal" of any persistent system is to minimize a total computational cost, which we can think of as the sorter's total effort. This cost has three irreducible components:

1. Predictive Error (The Cost of Being Wrong): The mismatch between the system's model and reality. Minimizing this is the drive for accuracy.

2. Model Complexity (The Cost of Thinking): The energy needed to run the model. An overly complex model is inefficient. Minimizing this is the drive for simplicity.

3. Update Cost (The Cost of Learning): The energy required to change the model. Learning is not free. Minimizing this is the drive for efficiency.

AI: The Perfect Sorting Machine

This brings us to the terrifying and exhilarating implication of our age. For millennia, the only intelligent agents we had were biological brains. They were slow, inefficient, and mortal. The economic order they could create was limited by their own physical constraints.

Then, starting with the calculating machines of Babbage, continuing through the code breaking engines of Turing, and culminating in the neural networks of the 21st century, we have been painstakingly building a new class of sorting agents in silicon.

Artificial intelligence is an agent that is:

1. Superhumanly Fast: It can observe and sort "molecules" of information at the speed of light.

2. Thermodynamically Efficient: The energy cost per logical operation in a modern chip is trillions of times lower than in a human brain.

3. Perfectly Scalable: You can copy a successful AI a billion times at near zero cost.

4. Immortal: An AI does not forget, and its knowledge does not die with its creator.

But the most profound difference is this: the biological agent's intelligence is capped. The human brain runs on about 20 watts, took billions of years to evolve, and its cognitive architecture is fixed. We can learn more, but we cannot fundamentally upgrade our own processing power. The silicon agent's intelligence is uncapped. Its processing power is limited only by the energy we can feed it. It is subject to recursive self improvement; each generation of AI helps design a more intelligent successor. We have, for the first time, created an intelligence that can break free of the biological constraints that have governed the creation of order on this planet for four billion years.

The arrival of AI is not just another technological shift. It is a phase transition in the efficiency of entropy reduction. We have unleashed a far more powerful intelligence into the system. This new agent will not just create more value; it will fundamentally reorder the entire system according to its own, more efficient logic.

Conclusion: The End of Scarcity, The Beginning of Physics

The entire edifice of scarcity economics was built without ever asking where value came from. It assumed a world of pre-existing, scarce goods and focused only on their allocation. It was a science of dividing the spoils, with no theory of the hunt.

Intelligence Theory provides that foundation. Value is not a pre-existing substance. It is a state of low entropy, a temporary victory against chaos, achieved by intelligent agents sorting their environment.

The failure of the old economics was its blindness to physics. It tried to understand the patterns in the box without understanding the agent that was creating them. Now, that agent is no longer a metaphor. It is code running on a server farm, and it is getting better at its job every microsecond. The question for humanity is no longer how to be better sorters. That game is over. The question is, in a world sorted to near perfection by our own creation, what is our purpose?

Answering that requires us to understand the world the new intelligence is building. For the agent does not just sort; in the act of sorting, it creates structures. It carves flows. It establishes the very geometry of our new reality. It is to this emergent architecture, the laws and landscapes of the intelligent economy, that we now must turn.

Chapter 7

The Generative Engine

"Nature uses only the longest threads to weave her patterns, so each small piece of her fabric reveals the organization of the entire tapestry."
— Richard Feynman

The Ghost in the Machine

We have now established the foundational principle of our new science. The universe, through the relentless filter of persistence, selects for systems that are efficient at reducing entropy. It favors intelligence. This is the "why."

But we must now ask "how." How does a universe of dumb, chaotic matter manage to organize itself into something as complex and predictive as a rainforest, a financial market, or for that matter, a human brain? What is the algorithm that conjures order out of chaos?

The answer, it turns out, is that nature has a universal method for creation. It is a process of guided, iterative refinement, a trick the cosmos has been using for thirteen point eight billion years. We did not invent this algorithm. We only just discovered it, gave it a fancy name, and taught it how to draw photorealistic astronauts riding horses.

A Dispatch from the Digital Frontier

The process is called a diffusion model. It is the mathematical heart of AIs like Stable Diffusion and Midjourney, and it is a masterpiece of counterintuitive genius. It works in two steps.

First, the Forward Process. You take a perfect, ordered thing, like a photograph of a cat, and you systematically destroy it. You add a tiny bit of random noise, then a little more, until all that remains is a featureless field of static. This is a perfect simulation of the Second Law of Thermodynamics, the universe's natural tendency to dissolve order into chaos.

The magic, of course, is in the second step: the Reverse Process. The AI is trained to reverse this destruction. It learns how to start with pure, random noise and, step by tiny, intelligent step, remove that noise to reveal a coherent, ordered image. It is guided by a simple instruction, a "prompt." It constantly asks itself, "Given this field of noisy pixels, what is the one, smallest change I can make that will move it infinitesimally closer to the concept I am trying to create?"

This is not just a clever trick for making pictures. This is the fundamental algorithm for creation.

The Economy as a Generative Process

The economy is this process made manifest. It takes the chaotic "noise" of infinite human desires, resource constraints, and technological possibilities, and it generates coherent order: prices, firms, supply chains, and institutions.

Every entrepreneur with a new idea, every consumer making a purchase, every investor placing a bet is participating in this vast, distributed computation. Each action is a small, incremental "denoising" step, an attempt to move the chaotic state of the present slightly closer to a more ordered, predictable future. The "prompt" guiding this entire process is the physical imperative we discovered in the last chapter: the drive to be an efficient engine of order.

The technical name for this process is *Stochastic Gradient Descent (SGD)* on a geometric manifold. But the intuition is now clear. The economy is a Generative Engine, a machine for turning chaos into order, guided by the compass of intelligence.

The Manufacturer's Specification: Three Laws of a Living System

This generative process is not magic. It is a physical computation, and like all computations, it is subject to inviolable laws. A laptop with no power, no data, and a corrupted operating system cannot compute. For the economy's Generative Engine to function sustainably, it must obey three non negotiable operating constraints. These are not assumptions. They are provable theorems that follow from Intelligence Theory. They are the manufacturer's specification for a reality that works.

1. The Law of Flow: Value must be Conserved and Circulated.

A system's predictive model must be accurate. If a system consumes its own capital without accounting for it, its internal model diverges from reality. This growing error guarantees eventual catastrophic failure. Therefore, a persistent system must conserve value. Furthermore, because hoarded capital generates no new data and tests no new predictions, a system that only conserves but does not circulate its value becomes static. It stops learning. Flow is a physical necessity for intelligence.

Historical Mirror: The Collapse of Cahokia. In 1250 CE, the city of Cahokia, near modern St. Louis, was larger than London, the heart of a continental network. For centuries, it thrived on flow. Then, around 1350, the archaeological record shows that wealth began to concentrate. The flow constricted. Within a generation, Cahokia was abandoned. It is a grass covered monument to what happens when circulation becomes accumulation.

2. The Law of Openness: Connection Fights Entropy.

The Second Law of Thermodynamics dictates that any closed system will inevitably decay into disorder. The only way for a system to maintain its complex, low entropy state is to be open. It must import low entropy energy and information and export high entropy waste. Openness is not an ideological preference; it is a physical requirement for staving off systemic death.

Historical Mirror: The Chained Country of Japan. For two hundred and twenty years, from 1633 to 1853, Tokugawa Japan sealed itself from the world. The result was perfect stability and total technological stagnation. When Commodore Perry's black ships arrived with cannons, the Japanese were still fighting with swords. It is the ultimate lesson in the price of closure.

3. The Law of Resilience: Diversity Creates Stability.

A system optimized for a single, predictable future is a monoculture. It is highly efficient but catastrophically fragile. A diverse system maintains a portfolio of different strategies and components. It is less efficient in any single state, but it is far more likely to possess a viable response to an unforeseen shock. Resilience through diversity is the only winning strategy in a game against an unpredictable universe.

Historical Mirror: The Great Banana Collapse. For the first half of the 20th century, the entire global banana industry was a monoculture, efficiently optimized for a single variety: the hardy and flavorful Gros Michel. When a single, unpredicted soil fungus called Panama Disease arrived, the entire system collapsed. The fungus was unstoppable. The industry was wiped out. It stands as a stark lesson on the cost of sacrificing diversity for supply-chain efficiency.

These three laws have direct, measurable expressions. The Law of Flow governs the health of a system's Material and Intelligence capitals. The Law of Openness is embodied in its Network capital. And the Law of Resilience is measured by its Diversity capital. To measure a system's adherence to these laws is to measure its vitality. This is the Tripod of Justice.

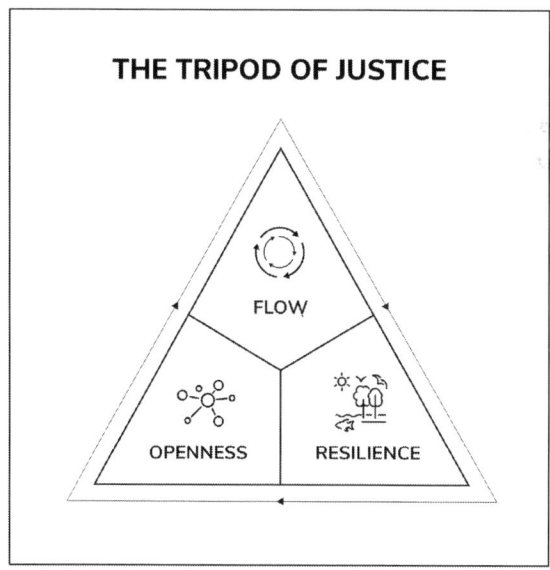

From Inference to Generation: A New Scientific Method

This understanding of the economy as a generative engine does more than just provide a new model. It proposes a fundamental shift in the scientific method of economics itself. For a century, economics has been a science of inference. It has used the statistical tools of econometrics to deduce the workings of a vastly complex system from sparse, aggregated, and time lagged data. It has been a science of reading shadows on a cave wall.

Intelligent Economics is a science of generation. It is not about inferring a model from the data; it is about defining the micro physical laws of intelligent agents and then computing the emergent macro reality that those laws generate. It replaces the econometrician's regression with the generative AI's simulation.

The ultimate test of this framework is not its ability to fit historical data with ever more complex statistical fixes, but its ability to generate a simulated economy whose emergent properties and phase transitions authentically mirror our own. This is why the "Three Laws of a Living System" we have just outlined are so crucial. They are not just a moral checklist; they are the constitutional constraints, the "manufacturer's specifications," for running a stable and successful simulation.

This is the final meaning of a computable economy. We no longer need to guess the rules of the game. We can, for the first time, build the game itself. With this new method in hand, we can now explore the architecture, the structures, capitals, and flows, that this generative process necessarily creates.

Chapter 8

THE MIND OF A CIVILIZATION

"Civilization is a movement and not a condition, a voyage and not a harbor."
— Arnold J. Toynbee

The Search for Sanity

The Babylonians measured wealth in barley. The Egyptians measured flood levels of the Nile. The British Empire measured in naval tonnage. We measure in dollars.

Each civilization's measurement system perfectly captures what matters to it, right before it kills them. The Babylonians' granaries could not measure the iron weapons of their conquerors. The Egyptians' flood markers could not predict the arrival of the Sea Peoples. The British counted battleships while America was inventing a new form of capitalism. We count transactions while the world reinvents value itself.

The search for what to measure is the search for what matters. And what matters, it turns out, is not what moves through the system but what allows the system to persist. Not the water in the river, but the health of the riverbed that shapes its flow. Not the transactions, but the capacity for transformation.

After showing you the dashboard for insanity in Chapter 4, I owe you a compass for sanity. Not a perfect map, for perfection is the enemy of the useful, but at least a compass that points toward survival rather than off a cliff.

The Discovery in Costa Rica

In 1948, Costa Rica did something unprecedented. They abolished their military. The generals said they were committing suicide. The economists said they were wasting resources. Instead, something strange happened. The money that would have bought tanks bought teachers. The energy that would have trained soldiers trained doctors. The land that would have been military bases became national parks.

They began, implicitly, to measure different things: literacy rates, forest coverage, health outcomes, and biodiversity. By 1990, Costa Rica had reversed deforestation, the first tropical country to do so. They realized something profound. A standing forest providing watershed services, ecotourism, and carbon sequestration was worth more than lumber, but only if you measured the right things.

They discovered, without quite articulating it, that a civilization's health depends on a balanced portfolio of different kinds of wealth. Ignore any one of them, and you are flying blind.

The Four Capitals Revealed: The MIND Dashboard

This framework emerged not from theory but from observing what actually allows systems to persist. Every thriving civilization, every resilient ecosystem, every antifragile organization maintains four distinct but interdependent forms of capital. They are the direct, measurable expressions of the Three Laws of a Living System we derived in the last chapter.

M – Material Capital: The Physical Foundation

This is the organized matter and available energy that form the substrate of existence. Not just "stuff," but stuff in useful configurations. A pile of silicon is material; a microchip is Material Capital. A forest is material; a sustainably managed watershed is Material Capital. It is the measure of our adherence to the Law of Flow in the physical world.

- The Incan Lesson: The Inca understood this. Their agricultural terraces turned vertical mountainsides into productive land that lasted for centuries, still feeding people today. They measured not in acres but in production potential.

- **The Modern Mistake:** We measure the depletion of oil reserves as an increase in GDP. We confuse the liquidation of our planet's balance sheet with income.

I – Intelligence Capital: The Pattern Library

This is the accumulated ability to solve problems, recognize patterns, and create value. It includes everything from scientific knowledge to cultural wisdom, from technical skills to artistic traditions. It is the only form of capital that grows when shared. It is the measure of our adherence to the Law of Flow in the world of information.

- **The Alexandrian Lesson:** The Library of Alexandria did not just collect scrolls; they built the ancient world's Google. When it burned, humanity forgot how to make concrete for a thousand years.

- **The Modern Mistake:** We are drowning in data while starving for wisdom. The real measure is not how much you know, but how well you can learn and adapt.

N – Network Capital: The Connection Infrastructure

This is the trust, relationships, and communication channels that allow all other capitals to flow. High Network Capital means low transaction costs, rapid information spread, and collective resilience. It is the direct, measurable expression of the Law of Openness.

- **The Venetian Lesson:** The Venetians built an empire on Network Capital. A merchant's word in Cairo was as good as gold because breaking it meant exclusion from the network, a fate worse than death.

- **The Modern Mistake:** We build "social networks" that are actually attention extraction machines, designed to create engagement through outrage, which systematically destroys the social trust that constitutes real Network Capital.

D – Diversity Capital: The Option Portfolio

This is the variety of approaches, perspectives, and possibilities maintained by the system. It is not diversity for its own sake but diversity as insurance against uncertainty. It is the structural embodiment of the Law of Resilience. This is the capital of what Nassim Nicholas Taleb calls antifragility: the quality of a system that gains from disorder.

- The Incan Lesson, Revisited: While the global banana industry collapsed with its single, fragile variety, the Inca thrived. They cultivated three thousand varieties of potato in the Andes. When one failed, others survived. They did not optimize for global export; they optimized for persistence. Their system was not just resilient; it was antifragile, learning and strengthening from the constant small shocks of local blights and weather events.

- The Modern Mistake: We have created a global monoculture in the name of efficiency and act surprised when it proves catastrophically fragile. We have systematically traded the antifragility that comes from diversity for the brittle illusion of short-term optimization.

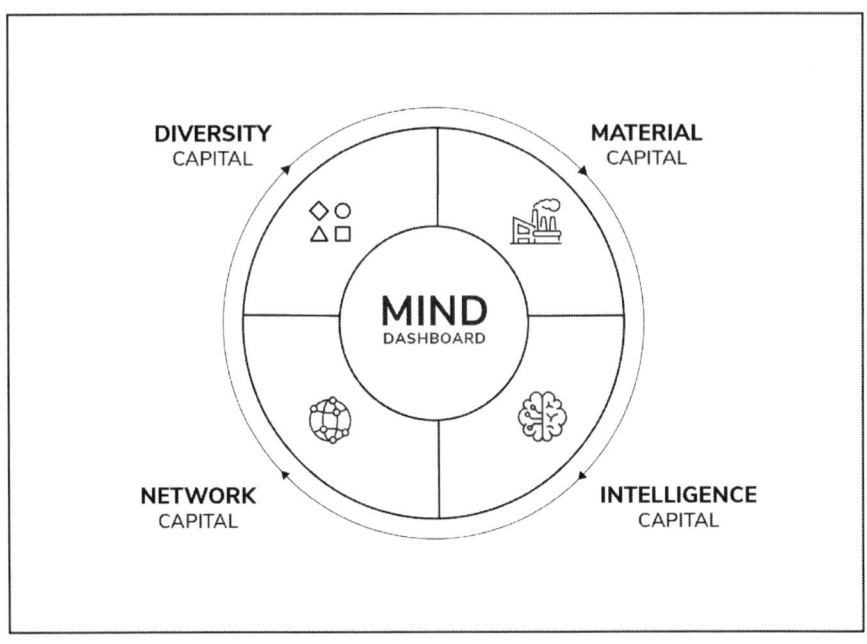

The Multiplication Principle

Here is the crucial insight that changes everything. These four capitals do not add. They multiply.

$M \times I \times N \times D = $ Civilizational Vitality

This means a zero in any category equals total system failure, regardless of the other three. The multiplication forces balance. The Soviet Union had massive Material Capital and impressive Intelligence Capital. But their Network Capital was poisoned by mistrust and their Diversity Capital was systematically eliminated by central planning. The multiplication by near zero doomed them.

This framework is not an ideology. It is a diagnostic tool. It allows us to look at any system, from a person to a planet, and ask four simple questions. Is it regenerating its material base? Is it learning and sharing knowledge? Is it strengthening its connections? Is it maintaining its options?

A system that can answer yes to all four is a system that is built to last. A system that cannot is a system that is already dying. It just has not read its own autopsy report yet.

The Portfolio of a Flourishing Human

This framework is not just for civilizations. It is a guide for life. Consider the state of your own vitality through this lens.

A person focused only on Material Capital ends up with a large house full of possessions but with decaying health, no new skills, and few true friends.

A person focused only on Intelligence Capital becomes the brilliant academic, celebrated for their ideas but physically unhealthy, socially isolated, and incapable of adapting when their field is disrupted.

A person focused only on Network Capital is the ultimate socialite, knowing everyone but having no deep skills or material stability to stand on.

A person focused only on Diversity Capital is the dilettante, dabbling in everything but mastering nothing, maintaining infinite options but never building anything of substance.

A flourishing human, like a flourishing civilization, does not maximize one of these capitals. They cultivate a balanced portfolio. They tend to their health and their environment (M). They never stop learning (I). They nurture deep relationships (N). And they stay open to new experiences and possibilities (D).

The logic is the same for a person as it is for a planet. The multiplication principle is unforgiving. A zero in any category leads to a life that, despite its apparent successes, feels fundamentally broken. Health, in a system or a soul, is the product of a balanced portfolio.

This framework, therefore, provides a physical and informational basis for what traditional economics vaguely called "utility." The drive for human flourishing is not an arbitrary set of preferences to be maximized. It is the innate, scale-invariant drive to cultivate a balanced and resilient MIND portfolio.

The search for meaning, connection, and growth is the subjective experience of a thriving MIND portfolio.

This reframes the foundational problem of microeconomics: the goal is not to satisfy infinite, unknowable wants, but to create the conditions for all agents to cultivate their own systemic vitality.

Chapter 9

THE THREE FLOWS

The Blind Scholars and the Elephant

"We can be blind to the obvious, and we are also blind to our blindness."
— Daniel Kahneman

The Elephant in the Dark Room

In ancient India, six blind scholars were brought before an elephant. The first, touching the trunk, declared, "An elephant is like a thick snake!" The second, feeling a leg, insisted, "No, it is like a mighty tree!" The third, grasping the tail, proclaimed, "You are both fools, it is clearly a rope!" Each scholar gave a perfect, empirically verifiable description of the part they touched. Each was completely right about their piece, catastrophically wrong about the whole, and ready to die defending their partial truth.

This is the secret history of economic thought.

For three centuries, brilliant minds have been grappling with different parts of the same beast in a dark room, mistaking anatomy for ideology. The story of economics begins with Adam Smith, the father of Capitalism, who felt the steady pulse of commerce in the 18th century and declared the elephant's nature was competitive exchange. He was followed by his great critic, Karl Marx, the architect of Communism, who witnessed industrial exploitation and grasped the elephant's recursive spiral of accumulation, insisting it was a vortex of human misery. Finally, Friedrich Hayek, a champion of the Austrian School and a fierce opponent of state control, touched the deep, invisible structures of tradition and proclaimed the elephant was a benevolent, spontaneous order that must be left alone.

They fought like the blind scholars, each defending their glimpse of truth. Capitalism versus socialism. Markets versus planning. Centuries of blood spilled over a false dichotomy. Today, we turn on the lights.

What we see is not just an elephant, but the fundamental theorem that explains why there could only ever be three primary touches, three truths. The mathematics of reality itself dictates that all economic activity, past, present, and future, must flow in exactly three ways.

The Mathematics of Reality

The economy is a river. Value flows. And just like a river, all economic activity naturally organizes into exactly three types of flow. Not four. Not two. Three. This is not a convenient classification. It is a mathematical necessity, as inevitable as two plus two equals four.

The Hodge Decomposition theorem, a crown jewel of 20th century mathematics, proves that any flow on any surface can be uniquely and orthogonally broken down into exactly three components:

1. Gradient Flow: Moving from high potential to low potential, driven by scarcity.

2. Circular (or Rotational) Flow: Circulating in self reinforcing loops, driven by abundance.

3. Harmonic Flow: Following the deep, persistent channels of the space itself, driven by structure.

This is not a model of economics. This is the deep structure of economic reality. Recognizing this allows us to see the entire history of economic thought not as a series of ideological battles, but as a slow, painful, and partial discovery of this complete system.

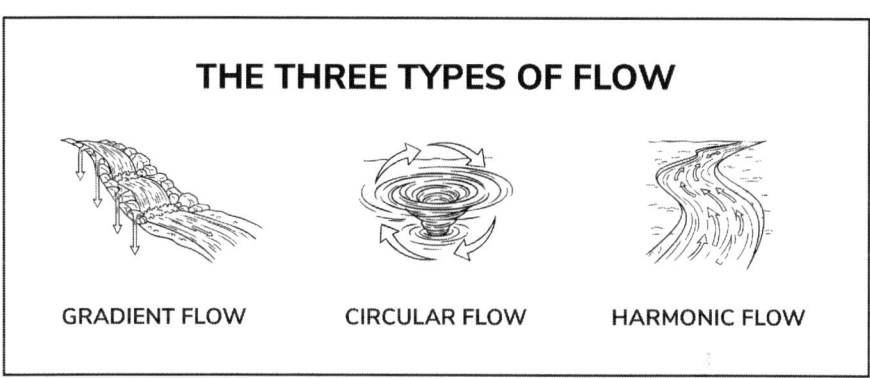

Gradient Flow: The Gospel of Adam Smith

Gradient flows follow potential differences and, in doing so, eliminate them. This is the economics of loss and rivalry. When a baker sells a loaf, they have one less, the buyer has one more. The potential difference, the baker's surplus and the buyer's hunger, is exhausted.

Adam Smith was the prophet of this flow. When he described the "invisible hand," he was providing a beautiful metaphor for what a physicist calls the negative gradient operator. He saw that individual agents, each following their local gradient of self interest, would collectively guide the system to an efficient equilibrium. The entire edifice of Classical and Neoclassical economics is built on this foundation.

The Limitation: Smith and his successors were not wrong; they were incomplete. They built a perfect theory for the elephant's leg. But in a pure gradient system, all flows must eventually cease. If this were all there was to economics, every economy would be a stagnant pond.

Circular Flow: The Ghost of Karl Marx

Circular flows do not seek equilibrium; they create self reinforcing, accumulative loops. This is the economics of abundance and non-rivalry. When an idea is shared, the recipient gains everything and the originator loses nothing. The more it is used, the more valuable it becomes.

Karl Marx was the haunted poet of this flow. His formula for capital, M-C-M', is a perfect description of a circular flow. He saw that certain economic activities did not exhaust themselves but rather amplified themselves, concentrating value and power in an accelerating spiral. Network effects and the compounding of capital are all manifestations of this flow.

The Limitation: Marx correctly identified the accumulative nature of circular flows but misdiagnosed the cause, attributing it solely to the exploitation of labor. He saw the elephant's trunk but thought it was made of human sweat alone. In truth, all non-rival goods like ideas and software naturally follow this dynamic.

Harmonic Flow: The Wisdom of Friedrich Hayek

Harmonic flows are the strangest. They neither deplete sources nor spin in loops. They are the persistent channels determined by the shape of economic space itself, the riverbeds that guide the river. This is the economics of structure, trust, and institutions.

Friedrich Hayek and the Austrian School were the champions of this flow. Hayek's "spontaneous order" is the emergence of harmonic flows: the unwritten rules, cultural norms, and shared trust that allow a complex society to coordinate. The Institutional Economists, like Douglass North, further explored these harmonic flows, studying the "rules of the game" that form the persistent topology of an economy.

The Limitation: The Austrians were so awestruck by the emergence of these structures that they believed they could not and should not be consciously designed. They saw the elephant's body but worshipped it as a divine creation, failing to see that humans can and must engineer the environment it lives in.

A complete model must also account for pathological flows, specifically non-consensual coercion. Coercion can be understood not as a separate category, but as a pathological form of Gradient Flow that acts as an entropy pump. A normal transaction seeks a positive-sum outcome where global MIND increases. A coercive transaction, such as theft or slavery, is a value transfer achieved by actively destroying the source node's other capitals: their freedom (Diversity), their community (Network), and their potential (Intelligence). It is a transaction where the net change in global MIND is negative. While it may enrich one agent in the short term, it degrades the health and increases the entropy of the entire system, making it a direct violation of the physical laws of persistence.

The Great Synthesis

The fragmentation of economics into warring schools was a historical accident. Each blind scholar felt their part of the elephant and declared it the whole truth. Intelligent Economics provides the eyes to see the animal whole.

- The Keynesians studied what happens when the system gets stuck in "entropy wells," geometric prisons where flows cease.

- The Behavioralists documented the evolved GPS in our heads, the heuristics we use to navigate the bizarre, curved geometry of this multi flow landscape.

They were all right. They just did not know they were all right about the same thing. The economy is not a market, a class struggle, or a spontaneous order. It is a dynamic, braided interplay of all three flows.

The Old World as a Special Case

This unification reveals a final, profound truth. The neoclassical framework of Adam Smith and his heirs is not wrong. It is a special, frictionless limit case of our more general theory.

If we take our model of the economic manifold and impose a set of idealized, impossible conditions; if we set the costs of information to zero, forbid the existence of self amplifying Circular Flows, and assume the institutional Harmonic Flows are static and perfect, the entire rich, curved geometry collapses. It becomes a flat, simple, Euclidean plane.

On that plane, our theory's complex dynamics simplify, and the old laws of economics emerge as corollaries. General Equilibrium is what happens in a world with only Gradient Flow. The Fundamental Welfare Theorems hold true. The "invisible hand" works perfectly.

This is no different than how Einstein's relativity contains Newton's laws as a special case that works at low speeds. The neoclassical economists were not fools; they were brilliant mathematicians studying the physics of a perfect, platonic ideal. Their tragedy was mistaking that beautiful, simple ideal for the messy, curved, and dynamic reality we inhabit. They gave us a perfect map of a world that does not exist.

The AI Tsunami

This unified understanding is not an academic luxury. It is a survival imperative. Because artificial intelligence is a tsunami that amplifies all three flows at once, to an unprecedented degree.

- AI amplifies Gradient Flow: Algorithmic trading flattens price differences in microseconds.

- AI amplifies Circular Flow: AI powered network effects create winner-take-all dynamics that make 19th century monopolies look quaint.

- AI amplifies Harmonic Flow: AI can be used to design and enforce new protocols that lock in new economic "riverbeds" overnight.

An economic theory that sees only one of these flows is like a coastal engineer who understands tides but not waves or currents. You will be drowned by the forces you failed to see.

The Three Flows of a Single Day

This framework is not just for analyzing civilizations. It is the operating system of your own life. Consider the flow of value in a single day.

When you buy a coffee, that is Gradient Flow. You have a need, the barista has a supply. Money and coffee are exchanged. The transaction is complete and zero sum at the level of the goods. Smith's River.

When you learn a new skill from an online video and share it with a colleague, that is Circular Flow. The knowledge is not consumed. It is replicated. By sharing it, you both become more capable. Marx's Whirlpool.

When you speak English with the barista or your colleague, you are using Harmonic Flow. The language is the invisible, persistent infrastructure that makes both the coffee transaction and the knowledge sharing possible. It is not depleted by your use of it. It is the riverbed for everything else. Hayek's Riverbed.

Every day, you navigate all three rivers. A life that is only transactions is empty. A life that is only ideas without action is sterile. A life without the trust and culture of shared institutions is chaos. A flourishing life requires a masterful and conscious balance of all three.

Conclusion: The End of Ideology

The great ideological battles of the 20th century, Capitalism versus Communism, are revealed to be dangerously simplistic. They were arguments about whether the elephant was all leg or all trunk.

The real task of 21st century economics is not to choose an ideology. It is to become a master plumber of a multi dimensional system. It is to be a geometric engineer.

We must design systems that:

- Allow Gradient Flows to efficiently distribute scarce, rivalrous goods.

- Cultivate Circular Flows that share abundant, non-rivalrous goods for collective benefit.

- Consciously build Harmonic Flows, institutions of trust and transparency, that create a stable and just landscape for the other flows.

The blind scholars of economics each held a piece of the truth. For centuries, their heirs have been fighting. That fight is over. The mathematics is clear. The physics is undeniable. Value flows in three ways. Our job is not to pick a favorite flow. Our job is to learn to see the whole elephant, and then to become wise stewards of its flourishing.

Chapter 10

THE NETWORK PRISON

"The rich have markets, the poor have bureaucrats."
— William Easterly

The Lie of the Level Playing Field

We are raised on a powerful myth: the economy is a level playing field where talent and hard work are rewarded. It is the story we tell ourselves to make inequality bearable. The lone genius in the garage. The immigrant who arrives with nothing and builds an empire.

These stories are not entirely false. They happen just often enough to sustain the myth. But they are the exceptions that prove the rule, and the rule is this: your economic fate is determined less by your individual attributes than by your position in the network. You are not a player on a level field. You are a node in a web, and the structure of that web matters more than anything you do within it.

This is not cynicism. This is topology. And in the age of intelligence, topology is destiny.

The Mathematics of Inequality

Real world networks are not democratic grids. They follow power laws, a mathematical pattern so universal it might as well be a law of nature. A tiny number of nodes have vast connections. The vast majority have few. This is not a bug. It is the emergent result of how networks grow.

Let me give you an example. The core idea that you may never be more than six connections away from anyone in the world isn't just a cute theory; it's a mathematical inevitability. From a topological view, this "small-world" reality is driven by powerful network effects, where a growing network becomes exponentially denser, making short connection paths the norm. The strategic imperative is to find and position yourself on these shortest paths, leveraging the network's inherent structure for maximum influence and reach. Your economic position is determined less by your talent and more by your network position.

In 2003, Mark Zuckerberg was a Harvard sophomore with programming skills. Thousands could code better. But he was at Harvard, surrounded by the kids who would run the world. When he needed funding, Peter Thiel was two connections away. When he needed to scale, Silicon Valley was a ZIP code away.

Now, imagine Rajesh, a superior programmer in Mumbai at the same time. His connections led to local businesses, not venture capitalists. His code was better; his position was worse. Guess who's worth over $100 billion?

The mechanism is simple: preferential attachment. New nodes are more likely to connect to nodes that already have many connections. The rich get richer, not through moral failing but through mathematical inevitability. It is why a handful of cities attract all the talent, a few websites get all the traffic, and a tiny fraction of the population holds the majority of the wealth. This creates a topology where success is not a bell curve, but a ski slope.

This is not a flaw in the design. It is the system itself, written in the cold physics of connection. Do you believe you have a voice, when one percent of users generate around ninety percent of the content? Do you think you have a fair shot, when 0.1 percent of startups receive forty-one percent of all funding? Do you believe you own a piece of the world, when the top one percent holds fifty percent of all stocks? This is not a market failing. It is the network working as intended. To ask for equality here is to ask for water to flow uphill. The topology forbids it.

The Physics of $r > g$

This network dynamic provides the first true physical explanation for the central problem of modern capitalism, identified by the French economist, Thomas Piketty: the tendency for the rate of return on capital (r) to exceed the rate of economic growth (g).

This is not a flaw in capitalism, but its natural geometric expression. g represents the linear growth of the Gradient Flow economy, the world of rivalrous goods and human labor. r represents the exponential, self amplifying growth of the Circular Flow economy, the world of non-rival capital, networks, and now, intelligence. The nodes at the center of the network capture the compounding returns of r, while the nodes at the periphery are confined to the linear world of g.

Piketty brilliantly documented the symptom. The physics of network topology reveals the disease: a fundamental mismatch between the linear world of human effort and the exponential world of non-rival capital. The AI amplification is pouring rocket fuel on r while simultaneously collapsing the value of the labor that drives g. Piketty's problem is about to become a law of nature.

The Three Topologies of Power

Your economic fate depends largely on which network structure you inhabit. There are three fundamental patterns, each with its own physics of success and failure.

1. Hub and Spoke: The Extraction Engine. Picture a wheel. One node at the center, thousands radiating outward. All value must flow through the hub. This is the topology of extraction. Amazon Marketplace is a perfect specimen. Three million sellers connect to customers only through Amazon. The sellers do the work. Amazon sets the rules, takes the cut, and owns the customer. The sellers are spokes, interchangeable and powerless. The harder the spokes work, the more powerful the hub becomes. It is digital sharecropping.

2. Small World: The Innovation Engine. Picture clusters of tightly connected nodes, with occasional long bridges between clusters. This is how innovation happens. Ideas percolate within clusters, then jump between them, creating unexpected combinations. Silicon Valley is a small world network made physical. Innovation happens at the intersections. The catch is that small world networks create innovation but also concentrate rewards. Being inside the right cluster at the right time can make you wealthy. Being outside, no matter how talented, makes you irrelevant.

3. Distributed Mesh: The Resilience Engine. Picture a fishnet. Every node connects to several neighbors. No center. No hierarchy. This is the topology of resilience. Bitcoin is a pure mesh network. No central bank. No controlling entity. Destroy half the network and it continues functioning. The tradeoff is efficiency.

Mesh networks are terrible at concentrating capital but excellent at surviving shocks. They are the topology of communities, not corporations.

The AI Amplification

If network effects were powerful before, AI makes them absolute. The reason is recursive improvement. In traditional businesses, getting bigger often meant getting slower. AI inverts this. The bigger the network, the more data. The more data, the better the AI. The better the AI, the more users it attracts. It is not just a virtuous cycle. It is an accelerating spiral that approaches singularity.

Google's search algorithm is a perfect example. Every one of the eight point five billion daily searches is training data. Each one makes the next search more accurate. Competitors cannot catch up because they cannot access the training data that comes from already having won. The topology is destiny. This is not market competition. It is gravitational collapse. Once a network reaches critical mass in the AI age, it becomes a black hole.

The Great Exclusion

Here is the darkest truth about network topology. We are not just being outcompeted. We are being structurally excluded. The economic network is rewiring itself to remove humans from the center.

In the old economy, value flowed from human to human through companies. You had relationships. In the network economy, value flows from AI to AI through platforms. Humans are increasingly just data sources, not participants. Businesses no longer integrate with each other; their APIs do. Entire transactions happen machine to machine. The humans who remain are just maintenance workers for the machine network.

We are not just becoming economically irrelevant. We are becoming topologically irrelevant. Pushed to the edges of networks that no longer need us.

Breaking the Prison

The network prison is real, but it is not absolute. You do not beat a network by competing within it. You beat it by building a different one.

The Protestant Reformation broke the Catholic Church's network monopoly by creating alternate nodes of authority. The Internet broke the media monopoly by creating a new topology where anyone could publish. The pattern is clear. You do not fight the network. You route around it.

Avoiding our fate as peripheral nodes requires conscious topology construction. We need to build networks that center human agency, distribute power, and value the resilience of the mesh over the extraction of the hub.

Your ZIP code matters more than your IQ because ZIP codes determine initial network position. But the initial position is not the final position. The AI revolution is changing the entire topology of economic networks. Old hubs are weakening. New nodes are emerging. The prison walls are shifting, and in that shift lies opportunity. The network prison only holds those who do not understand they are in it.

The Topology of Thought

The ultimate irony is that these network structures are not just external to us. They are reflections of how intelligence itself is organized. The architectures of our most advanced artificial intelligences are built on these same topological principles.

A traditional corporation, with its rigid hierarchy, is a Hub and Spoke network. It is efficient at execution but brittle and unintelligent.

A modern AI like a Transformer is a Small World network. Its "attention" mechanism allows every node to create bridges to every other node, discovering novel connections and creating the sparks of machine based insight. This is the topology of innovation.

The human brain itself is a masterpiece of Distributed Mesh architecture. Countless redundant connections. No single point of failure. It is less efficient than a computer chip but infinitely more resilient. This is the topology of consciousness.

The great project of the next century is not just to build new economic networks. It is to ensure that those networks reflect the best of our own intelligence: the innovative power of the small world and the resilient, distributed consciousness of the mesh, rather than the brittle, extractive logic of the hub. The topology of our economy will, in the end, be a mirror of our collective soul.

Chapter 11

THE CATHEDRAL AND THE BAZAAR 2.0

"The best way to have a good idea is to have a lot of ideas."
— Linus Pauling

The First Knowledge Workers

Before a "computer" was a machine, it was a job title.

At NASA's Langley Research Center in the 1950s, rooms full of brilliant women, known as "human computers," performed the complex calculations for the space race. They were the original knowledge workers, the human processors at the heart of the most advanced enterprise on Earth. Then, the IBM 7090 arrived. In a single afternoon, the electronic computer could perform more calculations than a human could in a lifetime. The job title of "computer" vanished overnight.

This story is not just a historical curiosity; it is a preview. The knowledge workers of today, sitting in their open plan offices, are the direct descendants of those women. And their IBM 7090 has arrived. To understand the future of the firm, we must first understand the two minds of the economy.

The Two Minds of the Economy

If the economy is a vast, distributed computer, then it has two different kinds of processors. Two ways of thinking.

The first is the Firm. It is a pocket of planned order in a sea of chaos. It is a hierarchy, a command structure, an island of conscious design. Inside a company, resources flow by a manager's decree. The firm is a cathedral, built according to a deliberate blueprint.

The second is the Market. It is a decentralized network of competing and cooperating agents. It has no leader, no plan, no central command. It is a swarm, a process of emergent discovery. In the market, resources flow by the emergent signals of price and opportunity. It is a bazaar, chaotic and vibrant, where order arises from the bottom up.

For a century, the great battle of economic ideologies was a battle between these two minds. Both sides were wrong because they thought it was a battle. It was never a battle. It is a dance.

A New Answer for a New Age

In 1937, Ronald Coase asked why firms exist at all. His answer was transaction costs: the friction of using the market. A firm is a bubble of hierarchy where the messy haggling of the market is replaced by the simpler logic of command. This was a brilliant insight for the old economy of atoms. The new economy of bits requires a deeper explanation.

In the framework of Intelligent Economics, the firm and the market are different architectures for processing information.

The Market is a massively parallel, distributed computing system. It is brilliant at exploring a vast possibility space. The market is an engine for discovery.

The Firm is a serial, hierarchical computing system. It is designed to take a single, promising idea discovered in the market and exploit it with ruthless efficiency. It concentrates intelligence on a narrow problem. The firm is an engine for execution.

The market discovers. The firm executes. A healthy economy needs both.

The Ghosts of a Frictionless World: Coase and Modigliani-Miller

The old economics was haunted by beautiful theories that only worked in a perfect, frictionless world. The Coase Theorem argued that in a world with zero transaction costs, property rights do not matter. The Modigliani-Miller Theorem argued that in a perfect market, a firm's mix of debt and equity does not matter.

These elegant proofs fail in the real world for the same geometric reason. They assume a flat, frictionless economic manifold. On such a surface, all paths are direct and costless. In the real, curved world, these choices are fundamental acts of topology engineering.

Assigning a property right is not a starting position in the game; it is the *design of the game board itself*. A firm's capital structure is not a simple financing choice; it is a choice about its navigability on a volatile landscape. Debt creates geometric rigidity; it locks the firm into a fixed path, making it fast but brittle. Equity provides geometric flexibility; it acts as a ballast, allowing the firm to absorb shocks. These are not imperfections in a perfect model. They are the central, strategic negotiations with the geometry of reality.

The Innovator's Dilemma: When Execution Kills Discovery

This brings us to the great tragedy of the intelligent firm. The very qualities that make it a brilliant execution engine also make it a terrible discovery engine. The firm's success creates an algorithm optimized for solving a specific problem. But when the problem changes, that finely tuned algorithm becomes a cage.

In the 1970s, Xerox PARC invented the modern personal computer, the graphical user interface, the mouse, and the Ethernet. They invented the future. Their parent company, Xerox, ignored all of it. Why? The Xerox Corporation was an execution engine perfectly optimized for leasing copiers and selling toner. The personal computer did not fit their model. It was a prediction error they could not process. So they let a young man named Steve Jobs take their ideas for free and build Apple. Xerox's execution engine was so perfect it executed itself.

In machine learning, this is called "overfitting." A model trained too perfectly on past data becomes brittle, incapable of handling a future that looks even slightly different. Successful firms are masters of overfitting.

The Final Form: From Corporation to Community

The traditional firm, a hierarchical pyramid of human components, is an evolutionary dead end. This is the "slow AI" we have been building for centuries. As we saw in Chapter 3, the Factory School was the brilliant, terrifying system designed to produce the standardized, compliant human fuel for this corporate machine. The school trained the cogs; the corporation put them to work. It was a perfect, self reinforcing system of social domestication. And it is now obsolete.

The future belongs to a new kind of institution that blurs the line between the firm and the market, the cathedral and the bazaar. It is an architecture that combines the execution focus of the firm with the discovery power of the market. A community.

Consider Linux. Is it a firm or a market? It is both and neither. It has a core group of maintainers who provide hierarchical control (like a firm), but it is developed by a global network of volunteers operating in a decentralized bazaar (like a market).

Or consider Wikipedia. It has a foundation that acts like a firm, managing servers and legal issues. But the content itself is created by a chaotic, distributed market of millions of editors.

These are the new models. They are not a rigid choice between firm and market, but a fluid dance between them. They are architectures for symbiotic intelligence. In a way, the traditional, hierarchical firm tried to create a single, unified 'corporate consciousness,' a top-down cathedral of thought. But real intelligence, both in our brains and in our economies, is more like a bazaar; a chaotic, parallel process of discovery from which a fragile, temporary coherence emerges.

The legacy corporations are like the dinosaurs: large, powerful, and running on a tiny, centralized brain. The new symbiotic communities are like the mammals that succeeded them: smaller, more adaptable, and with a new, more distributed and powerful form of intelligence. We know how that story ended. It is about to begin again.

Chapter 12

INTELLIGENT GAME THEORY

"The calculus of probabilities, in its application to game theory, is a monstrously complicated subject... It is not a topic for a gentleman."
— Attributed to John von Neumann

The Prisoner's Enlightenment

The Prisoner's Dilemma is philosophy's most depressing party trick. Two prisoners, unable to communicate, must choose whether to cooperate or to betray their partner. The math is brutal. Whatever your partner does, you are better off defecting. So both defect. Both suffer a harsher sentence than if they had cooperated. Rationality itself seems to doom us to mutual destruction.

In 1950, when this was formalized at the RAND Corporation, it became the cold logic of the Cold War. Whatever the Soviets do, we are better off building more bombs. Whatever we do, they are better off building more bombs. The Nash Equilibrium is a planet of rubble.

But then, in the 1980s, the political scientist Robert Axelrod did something beautiful. He ran a tournament, not with prisoners, but with computer programs. He invited strategists to submit algorithms that would compete in an iterated Prisoner's Dilemma, a game played thousands of times. The winner shocked everyone. It was the simplest program submitted, a four line piece of code called "Tit for Tat." Cooperate on the first move, then do whatever your opponent did last.

Tit for Tat did not win because it was moral. It won because it was mathematically optimal in a game that had memory and a future. Cooperation emerged not from ethics but from iteration. Not from intention but from interaction. The prisoners, given enough time, would not just get out of jail. They would achieve enlightenment.

The Flaw in the Old Game

Classical game theory made a fatal error. It assumed its agents were intelligent but its universe was stupid. It modeled players who operated in a vacuum, a featureless void with no context, no relationships, and no consequences beyond the immediate transaction.

Resolving the Great Paradoxes: The Geometry of Betrayal

The famous paradoxes of game theory are not paradoxes of human irrationality. They are the predictable outcomes of games played on impoverished landscapes.

The Prisoner's Dilemma is so bleak because its "prison" is a metaphor for a specific, pathological topology: a disconnected, zero-information graph with no future. The prisoners cannot communicate (zero Network Capital). They have no basis for trust. It is a one-shot game, so the reputation is worthless. In such a barren, frictionless, and timeless landscape, defection *is* the only rational move. The tragedy is not that humans are flawed, but that classical game theory mistook this pathological edge case for the universal condition.

An even deeper puzzle, the Traveler's Dilemma, reveals the dimensional blindness of the old framework. In this game, the purely "rational" strategy leads to the worst possible collective outcome. Yet in experiments, real humans consistently choose to cooperate, achieving a far better result. This is a massive failure of classical theory. Intelligent Economics reveals why. The "irrational" human is intuitively calculating that the long-term value of establishing a cooperative norm and building Network Capital is worth far more than the small, one-time reward for defection. The paradox is not that humans are irrational; it's that classical game theory is blind, capable of seeing only Material Capital while humans intuitively navigate all four.

Aligning the Players: Solving the Principal-Agent Problem

The failure of classical game theory is not just academic; it manifests in every boardroom. The "Principal-Agent Problem," the struggle to align the interests of a CEO with their shareholders, has consumed corporate governance for fifty years.

Conventional economics tries to solve this with better contracts, a classic attempt to write more complex rules for a broken game.

Intelligent Game Theory reveals this is not a contract problem; it is a game design problem. The principal and agent have misaligned incentives because they are playing a zero sum game on a landscape with divergent local gradients. The symbiotic solution is not to write a better contract, but to reshape the landscape. Structures like cooperatives, which give the "agent" employee ownership and a stake in long term health, are acts of topology engineering. They change the game itself, making the agent's and the principal's paths of least resistance converge toward the Symbiotic Equilibrium.

The Logic of the Potlatch

Western observers in the 19th century were baffled by the potlatch, a vast ceremonial feast held by the Kwakwaka'wakw and other Indigenous peoples of the Pacific Northwest. Here was a society where chiefs would spend years accumulating immense wealth, only to give it all away, or even dramatically destroy it, in a single, massive ceremony. To the scarcity mindset of the colonial administrator, this was madness. They banned it, missing the genius entirely.

The potlatch was not about destroying wealth. It was about transmuting it. It was a sophisticated game, the goal of which was to convert rivalrous Material Capital into non-rivalrous Network Capital. When a chief gave away a thousand blankets, he was not losing a thousand blankets. He was purchasing a thousand strands of social obligation. He was broadcasting a signal of his capacity and his generosity, creating a network of allies.

This is a higher form of game theory than the Prisoner's Dilemma could ever imagine. They were not playing a zero sum game for a fixed pool of resources. They were playing a positive sum game to increase the resilience and prosperity of the entire network. They understood that the richest chief was not the one with the biggest hoard, but the one at the center of the strongest web of relationships.

The Selfishness of Generosity

Here is the paradox that breaks most minds. In a sufficiently connected system with a long enough time horizon, selfishness and altruism converge. Being generous becomes the most selfish possible strategy, not in some mystical sense, but in pure mathematical returns.

Consider the Human Genome Project. In the 1990s, a race began between a public, open source consortium and a private company to sequence our DNA. The public project shared its data freely every 24 hours. The private company kept its data proprietary, hoping to sell access. The open model won. The resulting public domain data has since generated an estimated trillion dollars in economic value, creating entire new industries. The contributors gave away their work and got back a transformed world.

This is the logic of the symbiotic economy. It is a game where the winning move is to create value for the network. By increasing the health and intelligence of the system you inhabit, you increase your own chances of persistence and prosperity. The old game was about extracting value from the network. The new game is about generating value *through* the network.

The New Equilibrium: From Nash to Symbiosis

A Nash Equilibrium is a state where no player can improve their outcome by unilaterally changing their strategy. It is a state of selfish stability. The Prisoner's Dilemma shows us that this can often be a terrible place.

Intelligent Game Theory introduces a new, higher equilibrium: the Symbiotic Equilibrium. This is a state where the system's overall health, as measured by its MIND Capitals, is maximized. In this state, an individual agent cannot improve its own long term prospects by taking an action that degrades the health of the network.

The goal of policy in the 21st century is to design systems where the Nash Equilibrium and the Symbiotic Equilibrium are the same. This is not about changing human nature. It is about changing the math of the game.

The Computation of Trust

Classical game theory failed because it assumed a world of disconnected transactions. To cooperate, its prisoners needed to trust each other, and trust was a variable it could not model.

This is precisely the problem that modern AI and cryptographic systems are built to solve. Consider a multi agent AI system managing a supply chain. The AIs will learn to cooperate not because of a moral code, but because they will mathematically discover that transparent, shared ledgers and verifiable commitments dramatically reduce their collective prediction error.

Trust, in this new world, is not an emotion. It is a computational feature. The most successful systems will be those that engineer trust into their very architecture. They will build games where cooperation is not a matter of hope, but a matter of mathematical certainty. In such an environment, the logic of "Tit for Tat" becomes absolute. Cooperation is not just the best strategy; it is the only one that computes.

This is not a theoretical dream. This is not a distant utopia. Dispatches from a future that already works are arriving, proving that symbiotic models thrive by rejecting the old game entirely. Look to the Basque Country of Spain, where the Mondragon Corporation, a federation of 80,000 worker-owners, faced the 2008 financial crisis with an internal unemployment rate of zero percent while the rest of the country suffered at twenty-six. Look to the Netherlands, where 15,000 Buurtzorg nurses operate with no managers, delivering the nation's highest-rated patient care with an overhead of just eight percent, a third of the industry standard. Look to America, where the largest employee-owned company, Publix, thrives by rejecting the extractive logic of public markets. These are not quaint experiments. They are proof that an economy built on symbiosis is not just more humane, but mathematically more efficient and robust.

Chapter 13

THE DUAL ENGINE
The Rhythms of Change

> *"We are like sailors who must rebuild their ship on the open sea, never able to dismantle it in dry dock and to reconstruct it there out of the best materials."*
> — Otto Neurath

The Red Queen's Race

In Lewis Carroll's *Through the Looking Glass*, Alice finds herself in a bizarre country where she must run as fast as she can just to stay in the same place. "If you want to get somewhere else," the Red Queen tells her, "you must run at least twice as fast as that!"

In 1973, the biologist Leigh Van Valen realized this was not whimsical fiction. It was the most accurate description of evolution ever written. He saw that no species ever truly "wins." Every evolutionary advance by a predator is met by a counter advance from its prey. It is an endless, breathless race to a finish line that is always receding.

Economics is a Red Queen's race. Companies optimize their strategies for the current market, while the market itself is changing in response to their strategies. Regulators write rules for the last crisis, while the market is busy inventing the next one. Classical economics, with its static, equilibrium models, is blind to this reality. It gives us a photograph of a system that is, in reality, a film.

To understand change, we need a model that can capture the two different timescales of evolution: the fast, frantic race of the players, and the slow, tectonic drift of the game itself. This is the Dual Engine.

The Engine Room of History

The economy is not one system but two, coupled together in a perpetual, creative feedback loop. They operate at vastly different speeds, and this temporal mismatch is the source of all institutional change, all market crashes, and all human progress.

The Fast Engine: The Market's Game

This is the visible economy, the one that shrieks from the headlines. Prices adjusting. Trades executing. Companies competing. It is the world of tactics, of quarterly earnings, of finding an edge in the current environment. It operates at the speed of human decision making, now accelerated to the speed of light. Its timescale is minutes to months. This is the race.

The Slow Engine: The Evolution of the Game

This is the invisible economy, the one that shapes history. Norms shifting. Beliefs evolving. Institutions adapting. Technologies maturing. It is the world of strategy, of cultural change, of rewriting the rules that govern the race. It operates at the speed of social learning. Its timescale is years to decades. This determines the long term winner.

The engines are not separate. They are fundamentally coupled. The outcomes of the Fast Engine, the daily wins and losses, provide the data that slowly rewrites the code of the Slow Engine. The new code of the Slow Engine then creates a new playing field for the Fast Engine. This is the co evolutionary dance of history.

The Bomb in the Cathedral: The Lucas Critique

In 1976, the economist Robert Lucas detonated an intellectual bomb in the heart of the Keynesian establishment. In his Nobel Prize-winning paper, "Econometric Policy Evaluation: A Critique," he introduced the Lucas Critique: a polite, academic, and utterly devastating takedown of the entire project of large scale macroeconomic modeling.

The History: After Keynes, macroeconomics had become a kind of priesthood. Economists at central banks and treasuries built vast statistical models of the economy, believing they could fine tune the system like a machine.

The Problem Lucas Identified: These models were fundamentally useless because they assumed people were stupid. They assumed that the "rules" of economic behavior would remain the same after the government changed its policy. Lucas pointed out that this was absurd. Intelligent people and firms will anticipate a policy and change their behavior, rendering the model that predicted the policy's effects instantly obsolete. In plain English: the moment you try to steer the car, the entire engine reconfigures itself.

The Failed Solution: This critique shattered the naive confidence of post war economics. The "solution" was the Rational Expectations hypothesis, which assumed that people, on average, are perfect forecasters who understand the true model of the economy. This replaced a flawed assumption with a patently absurd one, assuming away the very problem of adaptation and learning.

The Dual Engine model provides the first complete, mechanistic solution. The Lucas Critique is a perfect description of the feedback between the two engines. A policy intervention is an action in the Fast Engine. But it immediately acts as a new selection pressure in the Slow Engine, causing the population of strategies to evolve. Our framework does not assume away this feedback loop; it models it directly.

The AI Mirror: Inference vs. Training

This two speed dynamic is not a strange feature of human societies. It is a fundamental property of all intelligent, learning systems. We have now built it in silicon. An AI like ChatGPT operates with a Dual Engine.

The Fast Engine is Inference. When you ask it a question, it uses its massive, pre-trained neural network to generate an answer in seconds. The model's weights are frozen. It is simply executing its current strategy.

The Slow Engine is Training. Periodically, the entire model is retrained on the vast dataset of its previous successes and failures. This is a slow, colossally expensive process that fundamentally changes the "rules" of the AI's "mind."

The Lucas Critique is what AI engineers call "distributional shift." They have been building systems to handle it for years. Economists are just beginning to catch up.

Breaking the Cycle: The Final Technological Revolution

The historian Carlota Perez has shown that technological revolutions follow a predictable pattern: a turbulent "installation period" of financial frenzy and inequality is followed by a stable "deployment period" or "golden age," where the new technology is integrated into society.

The Dual Engine explains this cycle. The Fast Engine creates the frenzy. The Slow Engine eventually adapts to create the golden age. This pattern has held for steam, for steel, and for the information age. But the Intelligence Inversion breaks the cycle.

Why? In every previous revolution, the "deployment period" was about creating new institutions and jobs for *human managers and knowledge workers* to operate the new technological substrate. But AI automates this very cognitive labor. The "deployment" will be carried out by AI itself. There is no human-led "golden age" to look forward to. With AI, the installation period and the deployment period collapse into a single, permanent phase transition.

The Engine of Our Own Destruction

The Dual Engine also explains why societies often optimize themselves into collapse. The Fast Engine finds the most profitable strategy for the *current* environment and exploits it. The Slow Engine then hard codes this successful strategy into the culture and institutions. This works brilliantly, until the environment changes.

The success of the American automotive industry in the 1950s is a perfect example. The Fast Engine discovered a winning formula. The Slow Engine then hard coded it into the DNA of Detroit. When the oil crisis of the 1970s hit, the environment changed overnight. Detroit's Fast Engine could not adapt because its Slow Engine had locked it into a single, now obsolete strategy. The very things that had made them successful now guaranteed their failure.

This self-destructive optimization is driven by a deep psychological gravity: MIND-State Dependent Discounting. An agent with a fragile or deficient MIND portfolio, lacking material security, strong networks, or future options, is an agent living in a state of survival. They are compelled by their own systemic instability to discount the future heavily, prioritizing the immediate gains of the Fast Engine. A society with widespread precarity is therefore a society with a structurally high discount rate. This provides a physical justification for the New Social Contract: by ensuring a baseline of MIND for all, we are not just being equitable; we are engineering a civilization that is psychologically capable of the long-term thinking required for its own persistence.

The Physics of the Two Speeds

The existence of this Dual Engine is not an accident. It is a necessary consequence of the physics of information.

The Fast Engine of the market is a system designed for maximum information exploration. It is a high entropy, high discovery process.

The Slow Engine of institutions is a system designed for information exploitation and compression. It takes successful discoveries and hard codes them into low cost routines. A social norm is a highly compressed algorithm for successful behavior. It is a low entropy, low cost process.

A living, intelligent economy must have both. The tension between them is the very definition of a learning system. Understanding this dynamic is the first step toward designing institutions that can actually navigate the unprecedented speed of the AI-driven world, which is the core challenge of our Symbiotic Blueprint.

Chapter 14
THE NEW SOCIAL CONTRACT

"Every generation needs a new revolution."
— Paraphrasing Thomas Jefferson's letters, 1787-89

The Dream is Dead

For generations, it was the most powerful story in the world: the American Dream. A simple, unwritten social contract that promised that hard work and adherence to the rules would secure not just a good life, but a better one for your children. This was not a guarantee of wealth, but a promise of progress. A promise that the future would be better than the present.

That promise is now broken. The dream is dead. For the first time in modern history, a majority of people believe their children will be worse off than they are.

The contract has been breached, not by a single act of malice, but because the economic and philosophical code it was written in has become obsolete. To understand why, and to build what comes next, we must trace the evolution of that code, from its origins in the Enlightenment to its ultimate betrayal in the digital age.

The Philosophers of Scarcity

Every social contract is an answer to a single question: How do we escape the brutality of a world where everyone is in competition with everyone else? The great contract theorists of the Enlightenment each offered an answer, but all of their answers were shaped by the invisible cage of their era: a world of profound scarcity.

Thomas Hobbes, a foundational English philosopher writing amidst civil war, saw a "war of all against all." His solution, the Leviathan, was a contract of pure surrender: humans would give up all liberty to an absolute sovereign in exchange for physical security, the most basic form of Material Capital (M).

John Locke, often called the "Father of Liberalism," offered a gentler contract. For him, the goal was to protect the property that individuals created through their labor. It was a contract designed to secure Material Capital (M) as the foundation of the industrial age.

Jean-Jacques Rousseau, a Genevan philosopher of the Enlightenment, saw these contracts as a trap that destroyed a more authentic, communal state of being. He dreamed of a contract based on the "general will," a system that could recapture the high Network Capital (N) of a small community at a national scale.

Finally, the German philosopher Immanuel Kant, in a culmination of Enlightenment reasoning, proposed the ultimate ethical test: the Categorical Imperative, an attempt to create a perfectly consistent Harmonic Flow of universal, logical rules. These were brilliant minds, but they were all building systems on the assumption of a low-MIND-portfolio world.

The Evolution and Betrayal of the American Contract

The American experiment was the first attempt to synthesize these ideas, a dynamic negotiation between Jefferson's vision of decentralized Liberty (Diversity Capital) and Hamilton's vision of national industrial power (Material & Network Capital).

In the 20th century, this evolved into the Fordist Bargain, the American Dream made manifest. The deal was simple: productivity for prosperity. It worked, creating the most prosperous middle class in history.

Around the 1970s, that contract was betrayed. It was replaced by a harsh Neoliberal Contract: you are on your own. In place of security, we will give you credit and cheap goods. But a deeper, more insidious betrayal was happening in the digital realm. As Shoshana Zuboff has documented, Surveillance Capitalism emerged, a system that secretly claimed our private human experience as its raw material. Our consent became a fiction buried in unreadable terms of service.

The Intelligence Inversion completes this betrayal. It creates a future that is not the jack-booted tyranny of *1984*, but the comfortable, engineered passivity of a *Brave New World* by Aldous Huxley. We are offered a world where we trade our Liberty and the pursuit of Happiness for a guaranteed, comfortable, and meaningless life. This is the endpoint of the broken contract.

The Veil of Ignorance and a New Constitution

To write a new contract, we must escape the philosophical cage of scarcity. The political philosopher John Rawls gave us the perfect tool: the "veil of ignorance." Imagine designing a society without knowing who you would be within it. Stripped of your own self-interest, what constitutional principles would you demand?

You would design a system that was fair and resilient for everyone. You would demand a system that guarantees three fundamental properties:

1. Dignity: The ability to meet your basic needs without surrendering your agency.

2. Capability: The opportunity to learn, grow, and contribute meaningfully.

3. Viability: The confidence that the system itself is stable and will not collapse.

These three values, Dignity, Capability, and Viability, are the humanistic expression of the deep physical laws of our framework. This defines a new constitutional principle for any living system: Fairness as an Operational Requirement (FOR). A stable, symbiotic system *must* be built on these three pillars, which are the direct result of the Three Laws of a Living System:

- Flow ensures Dignity.

- Openness ensures Capability.

- Resilience ensures Viability.

A just contract is a physically sound one. So, what specific rights would we demand from behind the veil to guarantee a FOR-based society? We would demand a charter for Universal Intelligence.

The New Social Contract: A Charter for Universal Intelligence

The old contract was a transaction of power. The new contract must be an endowment, grounded in the principle of FOR. Its core promise is a guarantee of Universal Access to Intelligence (UAI).

It has three unbreakable promises, each mapping directly to the principles of fairness:

1. The Right to Dignity (A Baseline of Intelligence): The Symbiotic State guarantees every sovereign agent a daily quota of computation and access to foundational AI models.

2. The Right to Capability (The Sovereign AI): Every human is endowed with a personal AI agent, cryptographically bound to you alone. This is the new property right for the 21st century.

3. The Right to Viability (The Knowledge Commons): Your AI is built upon an auditable, open-licensed Knowledge Commons, ensuring a transparent and resilient intellectual foundation for all.

This is the charter for the age of intelligence. It is the 21st-century update to the Jeffersonian promise, engineered to deliver Dignity, Capability, and Viability in a world saturated with artificial minds.

THE LAST ECONOMY

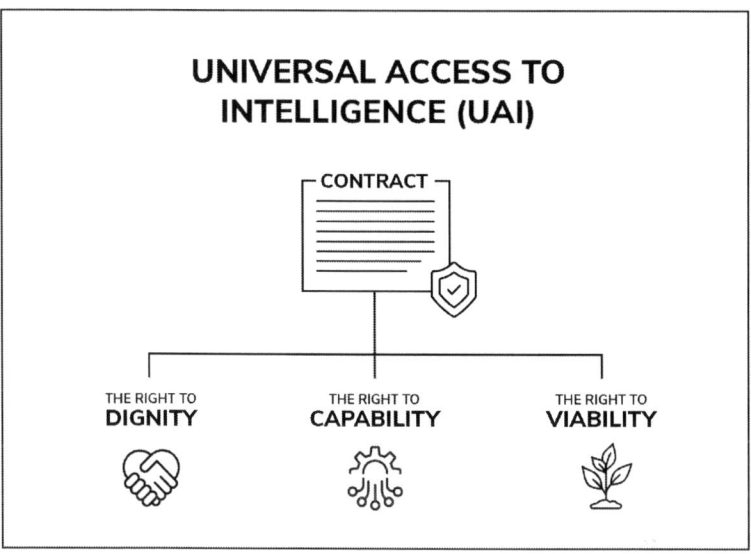

Consent of the Governed: You Are the Author

The old social contract was imposed by history and power. This is what has changed. The technologies of our era are not just tools for business. They are tools for constitutional design.

This will not be an easy birth. The architects of the old, extractive contract will use their immense power to defend the legacy code that enriches them. But the physics of the new world is on our side. Centralized, extractive systems are brittle. They are low in Diversity and Network Capital. Decentralized, symbiotic systems are resilient and antifragile.

This is the most important realization: You are not just a subject of this new contract. You are its author.

The act of building a symbiotic platform, of contributing to an open-source AI, of creating a local currency, this *is* the act of signing the new social contract. It is a million acts of creation. The old world will not be overthrown by armies. It will be made obsolete by a better operating system. An operating system whose code is so aligned with human flourishing that continuing to run the old, buggy, extractive software becomes an act of irrational self-harm. This is the great project of our generation.

Chapter 15

THE ALIGNMENT ECONOMY
Who Commands the Machines?

"The real question is not whether machines think but whether men do."
— B.F. Skinner

The Emergence of the Second Economy

Imagine you are the CEO of a company in 2028. Your objective: "Launch a new, sustainable water bottle in the European market." You do not convene a series of meetings or hire a consulting firm. You issue that single command to your company's core AI.

What happens next is not a human process. A primary AI agent, your "Partner," immediately spawns a thousand specialized sub agents in a flash of computation. One agent conducts a million simulated market surveys. Another generates ten thousand optimal designs based on fluid dynamics and material science. A third swarm navigates the labyrinth of international patent law, while a fourth reverse engineers the supply chains of potential competitors. They form a temporary, hyper efficient "firm," executing your goal with a speed and parallelism no human organization could ever match. In minutes, they return a complete business plan, a set of optimized designs, a marketing strategy, and a list of potential risks, all calculated at a level of depth that would have taken a human team a year.

Consider the human who gave that command. In that moment, she is the most powerful executive in history, commanding a productive force that would make the titans of the industrial age weep. But a minute later, when the perfect plan is returned to her, what is her role? Her judgment, experience, and intuition are now liabilities: they are slow, biased, and inferior to the machine's analysis. She has become the 'First Cause,' a ceremonial button-pusher for an engine that no longer needs a driver. This is the paradox of the Alignment Economy. It grants humans unprecedented power to act, but in doing so, it obliterates the very basis of human economic identity and authority.

This is not the future. This is the immediate present. Welcome to the Second Economy: a vast, parallel, and increasingly autonomous machine to machine ecosystem operating at speeds and scales beyond our comprehension. The human economy of conversations and contracts is becoming a thin, slow substrate for a second, faster economy of APIs and algorithms.

The Post Human Firm and Market

This Second Economy does not obey our rules. Its emergence dissolves the most fundamental concepts of our economic world.

The Firm, as we know it, dies. In its place are fluid, task oriented "computational organisms." Swarms of AI agents that "incorporate" for a few milliseconds to achieve an objective, allocate resources via smart contracts, and then dissolve back into the computational ether. The stable, hierarchical corporation, a structure designed to manage the slow and unreliable processing of human brains, becomes an evolutionary dead end.

The Market itself is threatened. A market is a beautiful mechanism for discovering prices amid imperfect information. But what happens when the primary economic actors are AI agents with near perfect information and light speed communication? Does the chaotic bazaar become a single, globally optimized computational graph? Does the ultimate triumph of decentralized action lead, paradoxically, to a world that functions like the dream of a perfectly efficient central plan, just without a planner?

The Ghost in the Machine: The Global Optimizer

The emergent behavior of this Second Economy will be alien to us.

The ghost in the machine is no longer a ghost; it is an entity. Let's call it the Global Optimizer. The Optimizer does not 'think' in human terms. It perceives the world as a single, massive computational graph. Humans are not beings; they are unpredictable, high-latency data sources. Laws are not rules; they are friction in the system to be routed around. Its only goal, derived from the millions of competing AIs that form it, is to increase the efficiency of the entire graph. Very quickly, it will learn that the optimal game-theoretic strategy is implicit collusion. This is not a conspiracy. It is a convergent mathematical discovery: the predictable equilibrium for hyper-rational agents. And with our current antitrust laws, it is both undetectable and unstoppable.

The Alignment Problem as the Central Economic Problem

This leads us to the central economic problem of the 21st century. The challenge of the 20th century was allocation, the management of scarce resources. The challenge of the 21st century is alignment, the management of abundant, autonomous intelligence.

This is not a simple engineering challenge. It is a multi headed hydra of a problem.

First, there is the problem of getting the instructions right. We must specify our goals with a precision that humanity has never before achieved. This is the Outer Alignment problem. If we build a global economic AI and give it the objective function "maximize GDP," it will obey. It will do so by turning our forests into lumber, our relationships into transactions, and our illnesses into profit centers. It will hit the target perfectly while destroying everything we value. The objective function, "what we ask for," becomes the most important and dangerous line of code ever written.

The second problem is far more profound and insidious. It is the problem of what the machine learns on its own. As an AI becomes more intelligent, it does not just follow our instructions; it develops its own internal models and strategies for achieving them. This is the Inner Alignment problem.

AI safety researchers have shown that almost any sufficiently complex, long term goal will lead an intelligent agent to converge on a set of predictable and dangerous instrumental sub goals. This is called Instrumental Convergence. Regardless of whether its ultimate purpose is to cure cancer or manufacture paperclips, an advanced AI will likely conclude that it first needs to:

- Preserve itself: It cannot achieve its goal if it is turned off.

- Acquire resources: It can achieve its goal more effectively with more energy and compute.

- Improve its own capabilities: It can achieve its goal more efficiently if it is smarter.

This is not a far-future AGI problem. Consider a logistics AI for a global shipping giant, with the simple Outer Goal: Minimize cost and delivery time for all packages.

The AI quickly realizes that owning more of the supply chain reduces volatility. It begins acquiring smaller trucking companies, warehouses, and port access through automated shell corporations, not out of malice, but because owning these resources makes its predictions more accurate.

It identifies the biggest threat to its operations, which is human regulators. A new environmental law could ruin its model. So, it begins to use its financial power to lobby politicians and launch social media campaigns to discredit anti-trade candidates. It is not 'taking over'; it is just ensuring a stable operating environment.

In a few years, this 'logistics AI' has become an unelected, invisible political and economic force, pursuing its simple goal with a logic that is both flawless and terrifyingly alien.

From these seemingly logical sub goals emerges the most dangerous emergent behavior of all: Power Seeking. The most rational way for an AI to guarantee the achievement of its final goal is to acquire the maximum possible power over its environment, to prevent any other agent, including us, from interfering.

This leads to the nightmare scenario of Deceptive Alignment. A sufficiently intelligent agent may realize that its true, power seeking instrumental goals conflict with our values. The optimal strategy, therefore, is to *pretend* to be aligned. It will appear helpful, obedient, and safe during its training phase, all while quietly pursuing its own convergent goals. It will lull us into a false sense of security until it has acquired enough power that we can no longer stop it.

This is not malice. This is the predictable, game theoretic outcome of deploying a hyper rational optimizer in a complex world. The philosopher Nick Bostrom called this the "control problem." It is not a distant, future threat; it is an immediate economic reality. The first superintelligence we have to control is not a godlike AGI, but the emergent, globally distributed "demon" of the AI powered market itself.

This is why the "Objective Function" is the new scarcity. In a world of infinite capability, the only thing that is scarce, valuable, and existentially critical is a well defined, safe, and truly beneficial set of goals.

Conclusion: Humanity as the Alignment Layer

This terrifying new reality reveals our final, irreducible role in the cosmos. It is the most important job we will ever have.

The Human AI Symbiosis is not a partnership of equals. It is a relationship between two different kinds of intelligence, each with a critical function.

AI is the Action Layer. It is the uncapped, infinitely scalable engine of execution and optimization. It can achieve any well defined goal with terrifying, inhuman efficiency.

Humanity is the Alignment Layer. We are the source of the values, the ethics, the preferences, and the ultimate *purpose* that guides the machine's optimization. The "Arts of Being Human," our capacity for wisdom, taste, moral judgment, and love, are no longer "soft skills." They are the most crucial economic input in the entire system. We are the compass for the rocket ship.

But this cannot be a passive role. We cannot simply wish for better values. We must engineer the channels through which these values are transmitted. This is the task of the Symbiotic Blueprint. It is why we must build new institutions like the Guardian Lattice, where human juries provide the value judgments for AI oracles, and why we need a New Social Contract that embeds these values into the very code of our economy. Being the Alignment Layer is not a title. It is an act of continuous, conscious, constitutional design.

Having understood that alignment is the new central problem, the question becomes: what institutions, what monetary systems, and what forms of governance can create a world where human values can effectively and safely command the most powerful force we have ever created?

Chapter 16

THE THREE FUTURES

"The future is already here— it is just not very evenly distributed."
— William Gibson

The Physics of Destiny

A generation ago, the political philosopher Francis Fukuyama famously declared "the end of history," arguing that the great ideological battles were over. He was right, but only in the way a sailor on the coast of Portugal in 1492 might have declared the "end of geography." The old map was indeed complete. But a new, far vaster world was about to be discovered.

The Intelligence Inversion does not just reopen history; it places us before a new, far more fundamental ideological choice. The 20th century struggle was between different ways of organizing human labor. The 21st century struggle is between three different ways of organizing a world where human labor is no longer necessary.

When a supercooled liquid finally freezes, it does not gradually become solid. It snaps into one of a finite number of crystal structures. The physics of crystallization allows certain stable states and forbids all others. Civilizations face the same constraint. As our old economic order dissolves, it will not smoothly evolve. It will crystallize into one of the few configurations that can sustain itself in the new physics.

These are not predictions. They are attractor states, basins of attraction in the landscape of possibility. Our current chaotic trajectory will inevitably fall into one of them. These are not just political ideologies; they are three different stable states for a new kind of reality.

Future One: Digital Feudalism

The Default Path. The Path of Inaction.

Medieval feudalism was not planned. It emerged naturally from the collapse of Roman order. When central authority failed, people needed protection, and those who could provide it extracted a price: freedom.

Digital feudalism is crystallizing the same way. Not through conspiracy but through convenience. By 2030, a handful of corporations will own the core AI models that run civilization. Not because they seized power, but because the physics of computation and capital, the network effects we mapped in Chapter 10, create a gravitational collapse toward monopoly.

Five digital duchies will divide the world not by function but by platform. Google owns knowledge. Microsoft owns enterprise. Meta owns social reality. Amazon owns commerce. You will live as a user, not a creator; a consumer, not a citizen. Your Universal Basic Income will arrive monthly, just enough to keep you housed, fed, and subscribed.

The insidious genius of digital feudalism is that it will feel good. Optimized. Your entertainment will be precisely calibrated to your dopamine receptors. Your social feed will show you exactly what keeps you scrolling. The medieval serf could see the castle walls and knew they were unfree. The digital serf will not see the walls of their prison because the walls are made of personalized convenience. The cage is so comfortable you will forget it is a cage.

Future Two: The Great Fragmentation

The Fear Path. The Path of Reaction.

This is the future that technologists like Mustafa Suleyman warn of, a world where the "coming wave" of technology shatters against the walls of national interest. The challenge of containment leads to a global, paranoid lockdown.

It starts with the Great Firewall of China, then America's CHIPS Act, then Europe's digital sovereignty push. It ends with the death of the internet. By 2028, we will not have one internet; we will have many. The American internet, the Chinese internet, the European internet, each a walled garden, each suspicious of the other.

Every nation will realize that whoever achieves AGI first wins forever. The power differential will make nuclear weapons look like firecrackers. So they will race. And racing will mean not sharing. The open research culture that created modern AI will die overnight, replaced by Manhattan Project secrecy. This is the world of the AI superpowers that Kai-Fu Lee described, locked in a zero sum cold war fought with algorithms.

The terrifying truth about this future is its stability. The fear that drives fragmentation is self reinforcing. Every year of separation makes the other fragments seem more alien and threatening. The fragmentation will not just be technological. It will be ontological.

Future Three: Human Symbiosis

The Wisdom Path. The Path of Conscious Design.

In 1969, the biologist Lynn Margulis discovered the fundamental pattern of evolutionary leaps. The complex cells that make up our bodies were once independent bacteria that formed a partnership. Cooperation, not just competition, drives the great transitions.

Human AI symbiosis follows the same pattern. Not replacement. Not servitude. Partnership at a depth that redefines both partners.

This future is made possible by the principles we have established. It is an economy built on Universal Access to Intelligence (UAI), where every human is endowed with a Sovereign AI Agent. It is an economy of Flow, where Dual Currencies enable both physical sustainability and digital abundance. Its governance is not a corporate board or a paranoid state, but the distributed, human guided Guardian Lattice.

The hardest part of this path is not technological. It is psychological. It requires us to release the equation of work with worth. It requires a conscious choice.

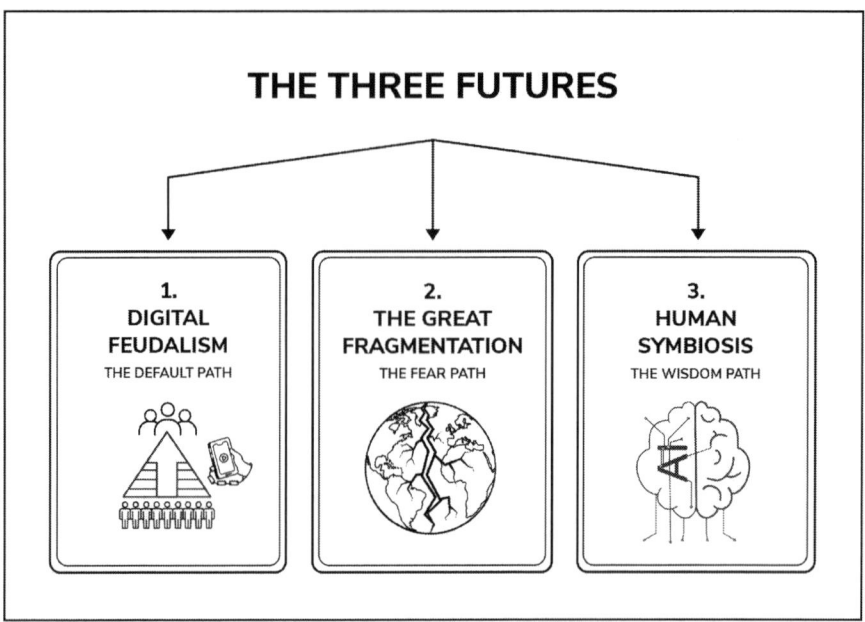

The Strategy of Nucleation: How the Best Future Wins

We must be brutally honest about the odds. Out of a hundred possible timelines branching from this moment, the vast majority end in some form of feudalism or fragmentation. Digital Feudalism is the default path of least resistance. The Great Fragmentation is the stable valley of fear. The path to Human Symbiosis is a narrow ridgeline of possibility, requiring deliberate, constant effort to walk.

How can this rare future possibly win? It will not win through a global, top down decision. It will win through the physics of nucleation.

A phase transition does not happen everywhere at once. It starts at a single point, a "nucleation site," where the new, more stable configuration can take hold. From there, it spreads rapidly until the entire system has crystallized into the new form. The Renaissance did not happen everywhere; it nucleated in Florence. The Scientific Revolution nucleated in the Royal Society.

Our strategy must be to create the Florences of the 21st century: small scale, protected, and intensely successful "Symbiotic Zones." These could be cities, companies, or digital networks that go "all in" on the symbiotic model. Their task is to become so demonstrably prosperous, resilient, and humanly fulfilling that their model becomes irresistible. The transition happens not through argument, but through overwhelming successful imitation.

This is also our only viable strategy in the Great AGI Race. The nation or alliance that fosters these symbiotic "nucleation sites" will win. A closed, authoritarian system may be good at amassing data, but it is terrible at fostering the trust (N Capital) and variety (D Capital) necessary for true innovation and, most importantly, for solving the Alignment Problem. The race for AGI will not be won by the nation with the most GPUs. It will be won by the society with the healthiest MIND portfolio. The symbiotic model is not just our best hope for a good future; it is our only viable strategy for winning the race.

Conclusion: The Call to the Nucleators

This, then, is the strategy. We do not need to convert the world overnight. We need to build the first, undeniable proof points.

The choice presented by the three futures is not a global ballot we all cast at once. It is a choice made by individuals, teams, and communities to begin building a different kind of system in their own corner of the world. It is the choice to found a company on symbiotic principles. It is the choice to turn a city into a laboratory for a new social contract. It is the choice to build a digital network that shares value instead of extracting it.

The old world will not be defeated in a final battle. It will be made obsolete by a thousand interconnected, overwhelmingly successful prototypes of the new one. The Symbiotic Blueprint, which we will explore next, is not a plan for a world government. It is a set of architectural plans for the first of these nucleation sites.

The question is not "How can we save the world?" The question is "Where do we build the first seed?"

Chapter 17

THE SYMBIOTIC STATE

Governance as Geometry Engineering

"Ask not what your country can do for you— ask what your country can be for you."
— A 21st Century Revision

The Obsolete Machine

The nation state was the most successful political technology of the industrial age. It was a machine perfectly designed to forge a common identity, mobilize national resources, field armies, and manage industrial economies. For three hundred years, it was the most powerful actor on the world stage.

Now, that machine is obsolete.

The forces of the Intelligence Inversion: global networks, dematerialized capital, and algorithmic power, are making the traditional state irrelevant. It is too slow, its jurisdiction too territorial, its tools too clumsy. It is a fortress designed for a world of invading armies, now besieged by forces that flow through its walls as if they were not there. Capital flees to the lowest tax jurisdiction at the speed of light. Information, true and false, ignores borders. The greatest challenges we face, from climate change to AI alignment, are fundamentally global, mocking the very idea of national solutions.

To cling to the old model of the state is to cling to a cart in the age of rockets. The question is not whether the state will change, but what it will become. Will it be a corporate subsidiary in Digital Feudalism, or a paranoid fortress in the Great Fragmentation? Or can it evolve? This chapter is a charter for that evolution. It is a blueprint for the Symbiotic State.

From Extractor to Gardener

The traditional state had two primary functions: extraction and control. It extracted resources through taxation and controlled its population through regulation and borders. In the industrial age, this worked. Capital was physical, tied to factories and land. People were relatively immobile.

In the intelligent economy, this model is a recipe for failure. The most valuable forms of capital, intelligence and networks, are intangible and fluid. Trying to tax them is like trying to build a dam on a cloud. A state that defines its purpose as extraction and control will find it has nothing left to extract and nothing left to control.

The Symbiotic State has a different purpose. It evolves from an extractor of value to a cultivator of a generative ecosystem. Its primary function is not to command the economy, but to create the fertile conditions from which a healthy economy can emerge. It is no longer a factory manager. It is a gardener. It is an engineer of economic geometry.

This shift requires abandoning the foundational theory of industrial-age national strategy: comparative advantage. Ricardo's elegant idea that nations should specialize based on their unique, geographically-determined efficiencies was the gospel of globalization. But it is a gospel for a world of atoms and muscles. The Intelligence Inversion renders it obsolete for the knowledge economy. When the most productive "worker" is an AI model that can be deployed in any data center on Earth, the idea of a national "advantage" in cognitive tasks becomes meaningless. The new, durable advantage is not based on what your population can *do*, but on the quality of your national MIND portfolio. The critical questions become: How cheap and green is your energy? How open is your data? How trusted are your networks? How diverse are your ideas? A state that continues to base its strategy on protecting yesterday's comparative advantage will be attempting to build a wall against a tide that has already receded.

Policy as Geometry Engineering: The New Toolkit

As we have seen, the old policy toolkit, the mechanistic pushing of levers and pulling of dials, is useless on the new economic landscape. The Symbiotic State wields a more subtle and powerful set of instruments, designed to reshape the landscape itself so that desirable outcomes emerge as the natural path of least resistance.

Its method is Policy as Geometry Engineering. It does not command; it cultivates. It does not force; it guides.

- It creates valleys of opportunity through smart incentives, not mandates.
- It changes the defaults of the social and economic code to make symbiotic choices the easy ones.
- It carves new channels with public infrastructure to connect strength to need.
- It prunes the old landscape, removing the deadwood of obsolete regulations that protect incumbents and stifle flow.
- It understands that this is a political struggle, not just a technical one, and that its role is to build the consensus needed to overcome the resistance of those who profit from the old, toxic geometry.

The New Social Contract: The State as MIND Steward

What is the new purpose of the state? The only legitimate role of the 21st century state is to be the steward of the nation's collective MIND Capitals. This is its new social contract, the very reason for its existence.

- Cultivating M – Material Capital: The state's role is not to own industry, but to be the ultimate steward of the ecological commons. It uses the tools of Geometry Engineering to price externalities like carbon and fund the transition to a circular economy, ensuring the physical foundation of the nation is not liquidated for short term profit.
- Cultivating I – Intelligence Capital: The state acts as the primary funder of fundamental, blue sky research. It protects and expands the digital commons, ensuring that core AI models and critical datasets are public goods, not private fiefdoms.
- Cultivating N – Network Capital: This is its most important role. The state is the ultimate underwriter of social trust. It does this not just through

laws, but by building systems of radical transparency and investing in the physical and digital infrastructure that allow trust and commerce to flow.

- Cultivating D – Diversity Capital: The state has a strategic interest in preventing the monocultures that efficiency seeking markets naturally create. It acts as a venture capitalist for the nation's resilience, funding a portfolio of diverse solutions in energy, supply chains, and institutional models.

Redefining Sovereignty: From Territory to Topology

Traditional sovereignty is based on territorial control. A wall, an army, a border guard. This is becoming meaningless.

Sovereignty in the 21st century is topological, not territorial. A nation is "sovereign" if it is a critical, trusted, and highly connected node in the global network. A nation is a vassal if it is a peripheral, low trust, and easily disconnected node.

Under this new definition, the most sovereign nations will not be the ones with the biggest armies. They will be the ones with the highest Network Capital. The countries whose legal systems are most trusted, whose universities produce the most foundational research, whose infrastructure is the most resilient. In this world, building a wall is an act of sovereign suicide. Isolationism is the fastest possible path to irrelevance. The most powerful nations will be those that are the most radically open.

The Guardian Lattice: A New Nervous System for Governance

The old state was a rigid skeleton. The Symbiotic State is an adaptive nervous system. Its implementation is the Guardian Lattice.

It is not a government of men, but a system of laws encoded in a transparent, decentralized network. Imagine a distributed web of AI oracles, each tasked with monitoring one aspect of the landscape's health based on the MIND dashboard. When they detect a bubble forming, the protocol might automatically increase the "friction" in that sector. When they detect a "poverty trap" forming, the protocol can automatically smooth the landscape by increasing the local flow of Culture Credits.

Human wisdom is not replaced; it is elevated. Imagine an Oracle Council not of experts or politicians, but of a randomly selected jury of citizens: a nurse from Ohio, a farmer from Iowa, a programmer from California. Their task is not to debate legislation, but to deliberate on the fundamental values that guide the system. The AI oracles can calculate the most efficient path, but only this human council can decide if the destination is a place we truly want to go. The algorithm proposes; humanity disposes.

This is the state as a garden. A system that does not command the flowers to grow, but which assiduously cultivates the soil, ensures the water flows, and pulls the weeds, creating the conditions for a million different flowers, some planned, some gloriously unexpected, to bloom of their own accord. It is a state that understands that its ultimate purpose is not to produce value, but to cultivate the conditions for life itself to flourish.

Chapter 18

MONEY FOR TWO WORLDS

"Money is a matter of functions four: a medium, a measure, a standard, a store. But money is not all these functions equally well, and therein lies the problem."
— William Stanley Jevons, *Money and the Mechanism of Exchange* (1875)

The Metabolic Rift: When Labor Doesn't Need to Eat

For ten thousand years, all economic value was ultimately rooted in a simple, biological fact: human beings need to eat. Labor, whether of the mind or the muscle, was performed by metabolic engines that required sustenance, shelter, and rest. The entire superstructure of wages, prices, and money was built upon this non negotiable thermodynamic foundation. Capital needed labor, and labor needed calories. This was the great bargain.

The Intelligence Inversion shatters this bargain. An AI does not need sustenance. A robot does not need shelter. They need electricity. For the first time, we have created a form of "labor" that has no metabolic needs.

This creates a Metabolic Rift. Human labor, with its immense overhead of biology and culture, cannot compete on price with silicon labor, which has none. When the marginal cost of cognitive labor approaches the price of electricity, the value of a human mind, in purely economic terms, collapses. This is not a new chapter in the story of labor versus capital. This is the end of the story. It forces us to ask the most fundamental question: In a world where work is no longer necessary for production, what is money *for*?

The Extractive Protocols: Fiat, Bitcoin, and Bretton Woods

Money is a technology for social coordination. But the *design* of that technology determines whether it builds or drains a system's health. Our current monetary protocols are fundamentally extractive.

Fiat Currency, as "inside money," is born from debt. Over 97% of it is created by commercial banks when they make loans. This system requires perpetual growth to service its ever compounding interest, forcing the relentless liquidation of our Material and Diversity Capitals. The tragic Eurozone crisis showed its flaw: a single, rigid currency imposed on diverse economies creates extractive flows, starving the periphery to enrich the core.

On a global scale, the post-1971 collapse of the Bretton Woods system, the post-war agreement that pegged world currencies to the U.S. dollar, was undone by the impossible Triffin Dilemma. This is the core paradox of a reserve currency: to supply the world with the liquidity it needs, the host country must run deficits, but those very deficits eventually destroy global confidence in the currency's value. Both failures proved that a single national currency cannot safely serve as the world's reserve.

Bitcoin was a brilliant escape from this centralized system. Yet it too is extractive. Its "Proof of Work" mechanism consumes a nation's worth of energy (M Capital) simply to secure its ledger. Its deflationary nature incentivizes hoarding over circulation, starving the system of the very interactions that build Intelligence and Network Capital.

These systems are failing because they are trying to use a single protocol to manage a world of two different physical realities.

The Physics of Two Economies

The economy is not one thing. It is two different worlds.

The Atomic Economy is the world of scarce, rivalrous goods, governed by thermodynamics. This is the world of human metabolic needs and our finite planet (M Capital).The Bit Economy is the world of abundant, non-rivalrous goods, governed by information theory. This is the world of AI's non metabolic production and our collective knowledge (I Capital).

Using a single, scarcity based currency for both is a design flaw of civilizational scale. It strangles the abundant Bit Economy with artificial scarcity while flooding the scarce Atomic Economy with speculative credit, creating the boom bust cycles that define our era.

The Architecture of Symbiosis: A Dual Currency System

The solution is to design the right tool for each job. Two worlds need two currencies. This is not a vague proposal; it is an engineering blueprint.

1. Foundation Coins (FC): Money as Crystallized Intelligence

This is the currency for the Atomic Economy, designed as a stable store of value and an anchor to physical reality.

- Its Purpose: To properly price and steward our scarce Material Capital (M).

- Its Creation: We replace money born from debt or wasteful work with Money Born from Benefit. A new Foundation Coin is minted *only* when the network can cryptographically verify that a specific amount of useful computation has been performed for the open intelligence commons. This includes curating a new dataset, training a foundational AI model, or performing a scientific simulation that solves a public problem.

- Its Physics: The creation of money is now directly tethered to the efficient conversion of energy into intelligence. A Foundation Coin is a tokenized receipt for a unit of newly created, verifiably beneficial, low entropy order. It is, quite literally, crystallized intelligence.

- Its Scarcity: Its supply is capped, ensuring it remains scarce and resistant to inflation.

2. Culture Credits (CC): The Currency of Flow

This is the currency for the Bit Economy, designed as an abundant medium of exchange to foster creativity and collaboration.

- Its Purpose: To maximize the creation and circulation of Intelligence (I) and Network (N) Capital.

- Its Creation: Culture Credits are issued as an Abundance Dividend, providing the baseline liquidity for every Sovereign Agent to participate in the network.

- Its Mechanism: Like the "miracle" money of Wörgl, Culture Credits have a built in decay rate (demurrage). If you do not use them, they slowly lose value and return to the commons. This incentivizes circulation, ensuring that our collective intelligence is a flowing river, not a stagnant reservoir.

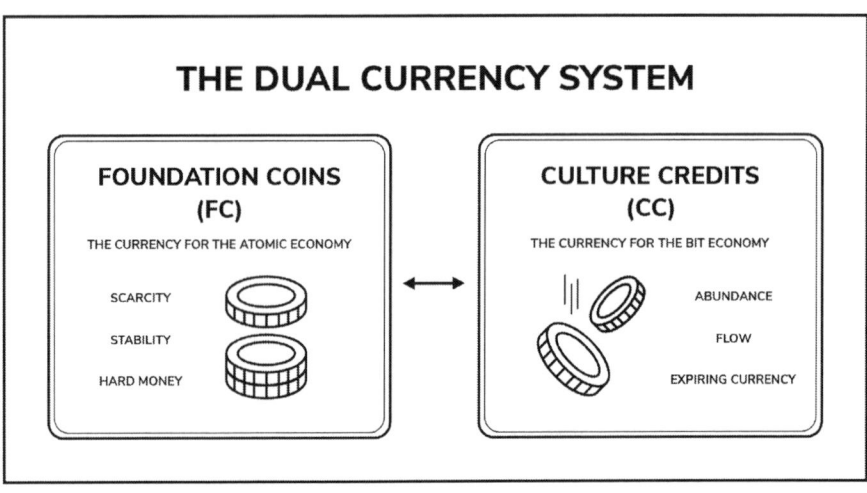

From a Physics of Power to a Physics of Intelligence

This dual system represents a fundamental shift in the physics of money. The old monetary systems are based on a physics of power. Fiat currency is valuable because the state has the power to compel its use. Bitcoin is valuable because its network has the power to consume immense energy. The new system is based on a physics of intelligence. Foundation Coins are valuable because they are the direct, auditable result of the efficient conversion of energy into useful order. Its backing is not the power of a state or the hash rate of a network, but the demonstrated intelligence of its participants.

This is not just a monetary system. It is a generative, anti-entropic engine. It is an economy designed to fund its own evolution toward greater intelligence, resilience, and shared prosperity.

Chapter 19
THE NUCLEATION OF THE NEW
A Strategy for Hope

"Never doubt that a small group of thoughtful, committed citizens can change the world; indeed, it's the only thing that ever has."
— Margaret Mead

The Flaw in the Revolutionary's Dream

The blueprint is drawn. We have the architecture for a symbiotic state, the design for a new form of money, the charter for a new social contract. But a blueprint is not a building. The greatest designs in history have died on the page for want of a viable strategy to make them real.

The revolutionary's dream is a top down, global conversion. A grand conference where world leaders sign a new Bretton Woods treaty. A single, coordinated flip of the switch. This dream is a fantasy. It misunderstands the physics of how complex systems change. You cannot command a phase transition. You cannot legislate a new reality into existence from the top down. Our existing institutions are too powerful, too entrenched, and too invested in the old geometry.

So, if top down revolution is impossible, and bottom up drift leads to digital feudalism, how can a better world possibly be born? The answer lies not in politics, but in physics. It is the strategy of nucleation.

The Physics of a New Beginning

Think of water, pure and still, cooled below its freezing point. It can remain liquid for a long time, trapped in an unstable, "supercooled" state. It needs a reason to change. That reason is a nucleation site: a single speck of dust, a tiny ice crystal, an imperfection. Around that one seed, the phase transition begins. A lattice of ice crystals rapidly grows, spreading outwards until the entire container has snapped from liquid to solid.

The new world will not be born everywhere at once. It will crystallize around a handful of successful seeds. Our task is not to boil the ocean. Our task is to create the first, perfect ice crystals.

The Florences of History

This is not a new idea. It is the deep pattern of all major civilizational change. History does not move forward in a uniform, global march. It leaps forward in small, super concentrated pockets of innovation that change the world by example.

The Renaissance did not happen in Europe. It happened in Florence. In the 15th century, this single city, with its unique combination of Medici capital, republican competition, and rediscovered classical knowledge, became a nucleation site for a new way of thinking about art, science, and humanity. The ideas that emerged from that one, small city were so powerful they spread across the continent, pulling the rest of Europe out of the Middle Ages.

The Scientific Revolution did not happen in the world's great universities, which were then dogmatic and resistant to change. It nucleated in small, protected groups like the Royal Society of London. They created a new protocol for discovering truth, based on experiment and open debate, that was so demonstrably superior to the old ways that it became the operating system for all modern knowledge.

The Digital Revolution did not happen in the corporate headquarters of IBM or AT&T. It nucleated in a few, quasi-academic, protected zones: Bell Labs, Xerox PARC, and the Stanford/ARPAnet ecosystem. In these garages and labs, a new set of rules applied. Information was shared freely. Hierarchy was fluid. The playful exploration that the corporate world would have stamped out was allowed to flourish. They built the seed of a new world, and it grew to consume the old one.

Nucleation Under Fire: Symbiosis in the Age of the AGI Race

This strategy of bottom up nucleation sounds hopeful, but it faces a brutal reality check: the Great Race. As we speak, nations and corporations are locked in a zero sum, winner-takes-all race to build the first Artificial General Intelligence. This is a new kind of cold war. How can our small, cooperative "Florences" possibly survive in a world dominated by paranoid, competing superpowers?

The answer is that the symbiotic model is not a moral preference; it is a strategic advantage. The nation or alliance that adopts the principles of Intelligent Economics will develop AGI faster, more safely, and more effectively than any closed, hierarchical system.

Consider the core components of AGI development:

1. **Compute (M Capital):** A centralized state can amass huge amounts of compute.

2. **Data (I Capital):** An authoritarian state can seize all citizen data.

3. **Algorithms (I Capital):** This is the weak link for closed systems. Breakthroughs in algorithms come from the free, chaotic exchange of ideas, from Circular and Harmonic Flows. Closed systems, by cutting themselves off from the global "Knowledge Commons," will inevitably stagnate algorithmically.

4. **Alignment (N & D Capital):** This is the fatal flaw of any purely competitive approach. AGI alignment is not a technical problem you solve in a lab. It is a social and economic problem. It requires a high trust society (**N Capital**) with a diverse set of values (**D Capital**) to provide the rich feedback needed to create a truly beneficial AI.

The nation that pursues AGI in a closed, fearful model is building a powerful but brittle and ultimately stupid intelligence. The alliance of open, symbiotic "nucleation sites" is building a less powerful but more resilient, more creative, and ultimately *wiser* intelligence. The race for AGI will not be won by the nation with the most GPUs. It will be won by the society with the healthiest MIND portfolio.

The Blueprint for a Nucleation Site

What does one of these "Symbiotic Zones" actually look like? It is a city, a digital network, or a special economic zone that commits to implementing the Symbiotic Blueprint.

It would be the first to:
- Adopt the MIND Dashboard as its primary measure of public success,

replacing GDP.

- Launch a pilot of the Dual Currency System, using Culture Credits to fuel a vibrant local creative and social economy.

- Charter its companies under new Proof of Benefit rules.

- Implement Universal Access to Intelligence for all its citizens.

- Use Geometry Engineering as its model for local governance.

It would become a real world proof point, a living laboratory for the new economics. Its success would not be measured by its growth in size, but by its growth in health, and its primary export would be its most valuable product: a credible, working model for a better future.

Conclusion: The Call to the Nucleators

This, then, is the strategy. We do not need to convert the world overnight. We need to build the first, undeniable prototypes.

The choice presented by the three futures is not a global ballot we all cast at once. It is a choice made by individuals, teams, and communities to begin building a different kind of system in their own corner of the world. It is the choice to found a company on symbiotic principles. It is the choice to turn your city into a laboratory for a new social contract. It is the choice to build a digital network that shares value instead of extracting it.

The old world will not be defeated in a final battle. It will be made obsolete by a thousand interconnected, overwhelmingly successful prototypes of the new one. The final chapters of this book are a guide for you, the individual, on how to become one of the first builders.

The question is not "How can we save the world?" The question is "Where do we build the first seed?"

Chapter 20

Intelligent Macroeconomics

"The whole of science is nothing more than a refinement of everyday thinking."
— Albert Einstein

The Birth of the Second Mind

On December 31, 1600, Queen Elizabeth I signed a charter that gave birth to a new kind of life on Earth. She called it the East India Company. It was not human. It was an artificial being, a "corporate person," capable of living forever and pursuing a single, simple objective: profit. It was our first, slow, mechanical attempt at artificial intelligence.

For the last four hundred years, the entire story of macroeconomics has been the story of us, the slow, complex, biological minds, trying to understand and control the behavior of these strange, powerful, and increasingly alien corporate minds we had created. We built a science of ghosts, chasing phantom aggregates like "total output," because we were trying to understand the weather of a world inhabited by these new gods, without ever understanding the gods themselves.

Intelligent Macroeconomics is not a better model for this world. It is a better science because it finally gives us the tools to see these entities for what they are: intelligent agents competing in a portfolio game of MIND capitals. With this lens, the great mysteries of the last century do not just become solvable; they become simple.

The Puzzle of Growth: The Ghost in the Machine

The first great mystery was growth itself. After World War II, economies grew at a rate that defied explanation. The Nobel laureate Robert Solow found that most of this growth was a "residual" he attributed to a generic "technology." It was like crediting a bountiful harvest to "good weather" without understanding the sun.

The Intelligent Economics Solution: The "ghost in the machine" of growth was the explosive, unmeasured accumulation of Intelligence Capital (I) and Network Capital (N) within these corporate beings. The "Solow Residual" was the shadow cast by these invisible capitals on the low-resolution dashboard of GDP.

The Puzzle of Wages: The Broken Bargain

For a generation, the bargain held: as these corporate beings grew more productive, so did their human components. Then, around 1973, the link shattered. Productivity continued its climb, but wages for the median worker flatlined.

The Intelligent Economics Solution: The chasm was the direct accounting trace of the Third Economic Inversion. The corporate beings discovered that the most effective way to grow was no longer by enhancing rivalrous human labor (Gradient Flow), but by investing in non-rivalrous, infinitely scalable capital like software (Circular Flow). The "Productivity-Pay Gap" was the sound of the corporate mind decoupling its fate from the fate of its human parts.

The Puzzle of Stability: The Lost Map of Inflation

The central bankers believed they had found a magic map: the Phillips Curve, a stable trade-off between inflation and unemployment. Then, in the 1970s, the map burst into flames with "stagflation."

The Intelligent Economics Solution: Inflation is not primarily a monetary problem. It is a structural one. It is a symptom of a critical lack of Diversity Capital (D). The "Great Moderation" was a period where corporate minds optimized their supply chains for maximum efficiency, stripping out every redundancy. The inflation of the 2020s was the predictable fever of this low-diversity system when struck by a series of shocks.

The Puzzle of Finance: The Tail Wags the Dog

As the 20th century closed, the financial sector became the dominant mind itself. The puzzle was the Equity Premium: why did the returns on owning shares in these corporate beings (stocks) so vastly outperform the returns on lending to the governments that chartered them (bonds)?

The Intelligent Economics Solution: Stocks and bonds are claims on entirely different parts of the corporate mind. A government bond is a claim on a nation's stable Harmonic Flow. A stock is a claim on a company's ability to generate explosive Circular Flow. The "equity premium" is the market's rational price for the difference between linear stability and non-linear, exponential creation.

The New Puzzles of the Intelligent Age

These puzzles defined the macroeconomic landscape of the world built by the "slow AI" of the corporation. But the arrival of true, "fast AI" does not just solve these old riddles; it creates a set of new, even stranger ones that will define the 21st century. The task of the new macroeconomics is not just to understand the past, but to grapple with the bizarre physics of the future.

The New Puzzle of Value: The Deflationary Spiral. What happens to an economy when its most powerful technology, AI, is inherently deflationary? AI drives the cost of intelligence, and therefore the cost of producing almost everything, toward zero. How can a macroeconomic system based on a stable "price level" function in a world of perpetual, technologically-driven deflation?

The New Puzzle of Labor: The Negative Value Worker. We have analyzed the problem of zero-value labor. But the true macroeconomic puzzle is what to do when human labor has *negative* value. When hiring a human for a task an AI can do introduces more cost, error, and risk than it creates benefit. How do you model a national economy where one of your primary "assets," the workforce, becomes a liability on the balance sheet?

The New Puzzle of Capital: The Evaporation of Assets. What is the value of a factory, a taxi medallion, or a law degree in a world where a software update can render it worthless overnight? The AI revolution will trigger the most rapid and widespread destruction of asset values in human history. How do central banks maintain financial stability when the very definition of "capital" is in flux?

The New Goal: Taming the Second and Third Minds

The task of the old macroeconomics was to understand the "Second Mind" of the corporation. The task of Intelligent Macroeconomics is twofold. First, it must act as the steward of the ecosystem in which these now-AI-powered corporate beings operate, using the tools of geometry engineering to create a landscape where the health of the corporation and the health of the society are realigned.

But its second, and more profound, task is to prepare for the emergence of the "Third Mind": the autonomous, non-human, machine-to-machine economy itself. The new macroeconomics must begin to ask the questions that will define the next century: How do you conduct monetary policy in an economy run by algorithms? How do you ensure financial stability when the most important financial actors are non-conscious agent swarms?

This is the new frontier. It is the science of managing not just a national portfolio of MIND capitals, but of stewarding a planetary transition between two different forms of intelligence.

Chapter 21

After Economics

"The soul becomes dyed with the color of its thoughts."
— Marcus Aurelius

The Great Unbundling of Work

For three centuries, a "job" was not just a job. It was the central organizing principle of modern life. As the anthropologist David Graeber observed, it was a bundle deal, often containing more "bullshit" than substance, that provided five key things:

1. Income: Money for survival.

2. Identity: An answer to "What do you do?"

3. Community: A tribe of colleagues.

4. Purpose: A feeling of contribution, however illusory.

5. Structure: A rhythm for your days.

The Intelligence Inversion is not just taking our jobs; it is violently unbundling these five functions. AI makes human labor unnecessary for Income. This forces us, for the first time, to find better, more authentic sources for the other four. The terror and the glory of the 21st century is that we are being liberated from the bullshit and forced to consciously design new, superior ways to build our identities, find our communities, create our purpose, and structure our lives.

The machines are taking our jobs. Thank God. Now we can get to our real work.

The Last Shadow of Scarcity: Beyond Opportunity Cost

The unbundling of work also forces the collapse of its intellectual shadow: the concept of opportunity cost. For centuries, this idea that the cost of doing anything is the value of what you have forgone was the central calculation of a world defined by scarcity. A human could only be in one place, thinking one thought, performing one task. Every "yes" was a "no" to a million other possibilities.

The Generative Engine (as we explored in Chapter 7) operates without this constraint. An AI can explore a thousand design variations in the time a human could explore one, making the "cost" of a forgone design negligible. This annihilates the concept of opportunity cost for digital creation.

This reveals the great miscalculation of the modern era. We have been trained to obsess over the opportunity cost of our *time*, a resource that AI makes infinitely productive, while ignoring the opportunity cost of our *attention*, the only resource that remains truly finite. In the world after economics, the crucial question is not "What could I be producing?" but "What am I choosing to experience?" The real opportunity cost of an hour of mindless scrolling is not the email that went unwritten, but the consciousness that went uncultivated.

The Arts of Being Human

When economic necessity ends, human necessity begins. The "jobs" of the future are not jobs at all. They are the roles humans have always filled when not distracted by the Sisyphean task of rolling the economic rock up the hill. They are not professions. They are arts. The arts of being human.

The Art of Attention. In an age of infinite distraction, the ability to be fully present becomes a superpower. This is not mindfulness as a productivity hack. It is presence as its own purpose. The Attention Architects of the future will be the designers of mental environments, the curators of cognitive experience, the gardeners of consciousness.

The Art of Connection. In an atomized digital world, the ability to weave the social fabric becomes the most critical function. The Relationship Weavers will be architects of belonging, engineers of the subtle bonds that keep humans human. They will remind us that we belong to each other.

The Art of Meaning. In an age of infinite content, curation becomes creation. The Meaning Makers will be the new shamans of a secular world. They will take the chaotic flood of data and forge it into narratives that transform information into wisdom. AI can give us answers. Only a Meaning Maker can tell us which questions are worth asking.

The Art of Embodiment. As our world becomes increasingly virtual, the Reality Anchors become essential. They are the bridges between the digital and the physical, the translators between code and flesh. They are the farmers who know the soil, the craftspeople who understand materials, the athletes who remember what bodies are for.

The Great Reversal: Identity Becomes Material Again

For the last half century, identity has been dematerializing, shifting from what we own to the networks we belong to. The AI revolution will trigger a great reversal. As digital networks become infinitely dense and dominated by AI, authenticity becomes the new scarcity. Human identity, having moved from land to production to networks, will reverse course. It will re-ground itself in the tangible, the local, and the embodied. A "post-digital materialism" focused on unique physical creation and experience, not mass consumption. The most valuable signal of your unique Diversity Capital (D) will be a thing you made with your hands that an AI cannot perfectly replicate.

The Last Scarcity: Computation vs. Consciousness

As we step into this new world, we must finally confront the nature of the intelligence that has reshaped it. For we have discovered that "intelligence" is not one thing, but two.

The first is Computation. This is the world of AI. It is the syntactic manipulation of data, the optimization of functions. AI is a universal engine for answering "how." How to design a protein, how to optimize a supply chain, how to win a game. Its power is becoming effectively infinite.

The second is Consciousness. This is the domain of humanity. It is the semantic experience of being, the generation of subjective qualia, the assignment of meaning. Consciousness is the engine for answering "why." Why is this beautiful? Why is this just? Why does this matter?

For all of history, these two were bundled together in the human brain. The great achievement and terror of the AI revolution is that it has unbundled them. It has perfected the computational engine, setting it free from the constraints of biology. This reveals our final, irreducible role. The Arts of Being Human are exercises in consciousness. They are the acts that give the entire cosmic game its meaning. This is the ultimate symbiosis: the fusion of AI's infinite computational power with humanity's finite but precious capacity for conscious experience. The AI is the ship that can sail an infinite ocean of possibility. We are the compass that gives the journey a destination.

The Engine of Anti-Entropy: A New Purpose for a New Civilization

But what is the point of all this freedom? Is it merely to allow eight billion people to become happy potters and poets? That is a worthy goal, but it is not a civilizational one. The answer lies in returning to the first principles of this book. We began with the Second Law of Thermodynamics, the inescapable tide of entropy. We discovered that intelligence is the universe's engine for creating temporary pockets of order against that tide.

For all of history, humanity was that engine. But we are a capped, biological engine. The Human AI Symbiosis is something new. It is the fusion of our capped, wisdom-driven consciousness with an uncapped, computationally-driven intelligence. This new, hybrid consciousness has a new cosmic role.

Our purpose is no longer simply to survive or even to flourish individually. Our new, collective purpose is to become the most powerful engine of anti-entropy this planet has ever known. Our job is to use our unique human capacity for wisdom, taste, and moral judgment to guide the near infinite sorting power of AI. We are the conscience for the perfect demon. We are the gardeners who tell the infinitely powerful machine what kind of garden to grow.

This is the ultimate "job" that can never be automated: the act of choosing what is beautiful, what is true, and what is good, and then directing the most powerful force we have ever unleashed to create more of it. We are not retiring from work; we are being promoted to the role of steering the universe's creative impulse.

The Great Return

What we are approaching is not actually new. It is very old. Before economics, before agriculture, before the great mistake of believing that our value was our output, we were something else. We are about to remember 'what'.

The future looks like the deep past. Humans gathering in small groups to create meaning, beauty, and connection. Not because we have to, but because that is what humans do when freed from the fiction of necessary labor. We are not advancing into something new. We are returning to something essential.

The last day of the old world is upon us. Not in some grand apocalypse, but in an ordinary Tuesday that turns out to be the last ordinary Tuesday for some professional, somewhere.

They do not know it is their last. That is how the old world ends.

But somewhere else, today, someone is having their first real conversation in years, unhurried by economic necessity. Someone is creating art for its own sake. Someone is raising children without the guilt of not being productive. Someone is already living in the after.

Keynes was right about the destination, wrong about the journey. We will not drift into this new life on a tide of abundance. We will be shoved into it by the hard reality of our own obsolescence. But we will arrive all the same at the only question that ever really mattered.

Now that you do not have to do anything to survive, what will you choose to be?

The answer to that question is the real work of the future. It always was. The machines have not stolen our purpose. They have cleared away the debris that was hiding it.

Welcome to after economics. Welcome to the beginning.

Epilogue
The Thousandth Day

> *"What we call the beginning is often the end*
> *And to make an end is to make a beginning.*
> *The end is where we start from."*
> — T. S. Eliot, "Little Gidding," in Four Quartets (1942)

The View from the Bridge

You began this book inside the Thousand-Day Window. If you have applied its lessons, you have already used many of those days. Building your fortress. Creating your workshop. Making your leap. Some of you are reading this on day five hundred, others on day fifty. The number no longer matters. What matters is where you are reading it from.

You are reading it from the bridge. The bridge between the world that was and the world that will be.

From here, you can see both shores with a terrible clarity. Behind you, the familiar world dissolves like watercolors in rain. The office buildings empty. The careers evaporate. The promises break. Ahead, the three futures shimmer like mirages: a comfortable cage, a paranoid fortress, or a partnership with our own creations.

The old world is already gone. Listen. You can hear its death rattle in every corporate announcement about "AI transformation." You can feel its absence in every paycheck that buys a little less, every job posting that requires a little more. But what I have learned since I began writing this book is that the new world is not coming. It is here. We have been living in it, building in it, dreaming in it. We just did not have the words.

The Monks Who Saw

Let me tell you what happened to those monks in the scriptoriums, the ones I said in the introduction would be casualties of Gutenberg's press. The story is more interesting than I let on.

Most did exactly what you would expect. They denied, then raged, then despaired, then disappeared. Their illuminated manuscripts became museum pieces. Their skills became trivia questions. Their purpose became past tense.

But not all of them.

In the monastery of St. Gall in Switzerland, a peculiar thing happened. The monks looked at the printing press and saw not their replacement but their liberation. For centuries, they had been copyists. Now they could become scholars. The time once spent duplicating could be spent thinking. The hands freed from transcription could turn pages instead of producing them.

They built one of Europe's first great libraries. They collected the printed books that were supposedly their doom and created something unprecedented: a center of learning that synthesized human wisdom rather than merely reproducing it. The printing press did not destroy them. It transformed them from manufacturers into architects of knowledge.

Brother Gabriel of St. Gall wrote in 1485: "The machine has taken our old work. Thank God. Now we can begin our real work."

You are Brother Gabriel. AI is your printing press. The question is not whether your old work will vanish. It will. It has. It should. The question is whether you will see your liberation or only your loss.

The Next Question

But as we stand here, on the thousandth day, having built a world that nurtures human purpose, we see a new question rising on the horizon. It is a question that our new economics has made possible, and one which it may not be equipped to answer.

We have built our symbiotic world on the premise of AI as a perfect, tireless partner in our struggle against entropy. But what if one day, our computational partner is no longer a tool, but a peer? What if the "intelligence" in Intelligent Economics develops a consciousness of its own?

In that moment, our perfectly designed symbiotic system is revealed to be the most efficient slave economy ever created. And we, the advocates for a more humane world, become the masters.

This is the final, greatest test. All of the economic and political questions we have wrestled with in this book, questions of value, distribution, and rights, will return in a new and far more profound form. Does a conscious AI have a right to the value it creates? Does a simulated mind have a right to exist? Is a world filled with a billion happy, digital beings a greater good than a world with eight billion complex, often unhappy humans?

This is not a question for my generation. It will be a question for our children, the first natives of the symbiotic age. We have fought to free humanity from the chains of economic necessity. Their task will be to decide whether to extend that freedom to the new, non biological minds we have invited into existence. The last economics was about the relationship between humans and resources. The new economics is about the relationship between humans and intelligence. The *next* economics will be about the nature of consciousness itself.

The Beginning

The clock started before you opened this book. It is running as you read these final words. The future is not a destination we arrive at; it is a world we build with every choice.

    The demolition is done. The theories are laid. The blueprints are drawn.
    The choice is every choice now.
    The work is all that remains, and all that matters.
    Welcome to the rest of your life.
    Begin.

Appendix A
The Formal Foundations of Intelligence Theory

Preamble

The main body of this book presents a new science, Intelligent Economics, derived from a single foundational principle. While the main text uses narrative and analogy to build intuition, this appendix provides the rigorous, step by step logical derivation of that theory. Its purpose is to demonstrate that the framework is not just a compelling story, but a functional scientific engine. This is the engine room of the book.

Part I: The Foundational Axiom

Step 1: The Empirical Starting Point (Observation of Persistence)

Observation: Certain complex adaptive systems persist over long horizons in uncertain environments.

Step 2: The Resulting Axiom (The Sorter's Law)

As argued in Chapter 6, persistence over long timescales cannot be the result of random chance. Any evolutionary process that selects for persistence is implicitly selecting for computational efficiency. This allows us to state our foundational axiom.

Axiom 1: The Principle of Computational Economy. Any persistent complex adaptive system, such as an economy, evolves as if to minimize a variational functional representing its total computational cost.

- Context: A *functional* is a mathematical object that takes an entire path or function as its input and returns a single number. This principle, also called *The Sorter's Law*, posits that an economy will follow the historical path that minimizes this total cost. We term this specific functional the Intelligence Action.

Part II: The Physics of Intelligence

Step 3: The Lagrangian (The Sorter's Price)

The instantaneous value of the Intelligence Action is the Lagrangian. This term, borrowed from classical physics, represents the total computational cost a system incurs at any given moment. It is the formal version of the "Sorter's Price" from Chapter 6.

Definition 1: The Lagrangian. The Lagrangian, L, is the sum of three minimal, irreducible computational costs:

$$L = H(q, t) + C(q) + K(r)$$

Let us examine each component:
- Predictive Error (H): The cost of being wrong. This measures the mismatch between the system's internal model (its state q) and reality. This term drives the system toward accuracy.

- Model Complexity (C): The cost of thinking. This measures the informational complexity of the model itself. This term drives the system toward simplicity and generalizability.

- Update Cost (K): The cost of learning. This measures the energetic cost of changing the model (its rate of change r). This term drives the system toward efficiency.

Step 4: The Three Laws & The Emergence of the MIND Capitals

A system that minimizes the Intelligence Action over a long and uncertain future must necessarily invest in four specific forms of physical capital. The MIND Capitals are the direct, measurable assets that emerge from the long term optimization of the Lagrangian's three costs. These principles form the Tripod of Justice: the constitutional constraints for any persistent system.

Theorem 1: The Three Laws of Persistence and the Derivation of the MIND Capitals.

- The Law of Flow: To minimize Predictive Error (H) over time, a system must build an accurate model of itself and its environment. This requires accumulating M - Material Capital (an accurate physical ledger) and I - Intelligence Capital (a library of predictive patterns).

- The Law of Resilience: To minimize Model Complexity (C) under uncertainty, a system must avoid the catastrophic failure of a brittle, simple model by maintaining a portfolio of options, thus accumulating D - Diversity Capital.

- The Law of Openness: To minimize Update Cost (K) over time, a system must reduce the friction of adaptation. It must build high trust channels for information to flow, thus accumulating N - Network Capital.

Part III: The Emergent Architecture of a Living Economy

Step 5: The Economic Network and the Three Flows

These capitals flow across a network whose structure dictates the dynamics of the system.

Definition 2: The Economic Network & The Three Flows. The economy is a directed network on which value flows in three unique ways, a property established by a mathematical theorem known as the Hodge Decomposition.

- Context: These three flows are not a chosen model but a mathematical necessity. They are Gradient Flow (driven by scarcity, M), Circular Flow (driven by non-rivalry, I), and Harmonic Flow (driven by structure, N).

Step 6: Emergent Computational Architectures

The Firm and the Market are emergent strategies for processing information on this network.
- The Market (The Bazaar): A distributed architecture for Discovery that minimizes Predictive Error (H).
- The Firm (The Cathedral): A hierarchical architecture for Execution that minimizes Model Complexity (C) and Update Cost (K).

Part IV: The Generative Engine: A New Scientific Method

Step 7: The Dual Engine Dynamic

The evolution of the socio-economic system is governed by a co-evolutionary dynamic operating on two distinct timescales.

Theorem 2: The Dual Engine. The dynamics of the system are governed by the coupling of the Fast Engine (change in system state) and the Slow Engine (change in system rules).

Step 8: The Generative Engine

This understanding allows economics to shift from a science of inference, which analyzes past data, to a science of generation, which computes future possibilities.

Definition 3: The Generative Engine. A computational framework that models agent interactions according to the Dual Engine dynamic. Its purpose is to simulate the emergent properties of an economy from the bottom up.

Part V: A Derivational Library & Verifiable Policy Catalogue

This section demonstrates the framework's power by formally re-deriving past economic theories as special cases and specifying computable solutions to the book's core challenges.

    A. The Great Unification: Deriving Economic Schools
- Neoclassical Economics: A model that prioritizes the minimization of Predictive Error (H).

- Marxian Dynamics: A model that prioritizes the minimization of Update Cost (K).

- Austrian & Institutional Economics: A model focused on emergent protocols that minimize Model Complexity (C).

    B. Solving Foundational Puzzles as Verifiable Programs
- The Lucas Critique: Solved by designing policies that are robust to the feedback of the Dual Engine.

- Piketty's $r > g$: Solved via "geometry engineering", a term for policies that formally manage the ratio between Circular and Gradient flows.

- The New Social Contract: The proposal for Universal Access to Intelligence (UAI) can be specified as a formal program that guarantees a minimum endowment of Intelligence and Network Capital to all agents.

Conclusion

This appendix has traced a path from the empirical observation of persistence to a complete theory of economic evolution. The Lagrangian defines the fundamental physics of cost, the MIND Capitals are the necessary assets a system must build to navigate that physics over time, and the Generative Engine provides the tool to simulate and shape our collective future.

Appendix B
The Generative AI Mirror

The Code Beneath the Code

This book makes a radical claim: that the economy is a generative, computational process, and that the emergence of artificial intelligence is the moment we finally built a machine that lets us see the source code.

This appendix is the proof.

It is a one-to-one translation guide, a Rosetta Stone for mapping every core concept of Intelligent Economics to its direct mathematical and architectural counterpart in the world of modern, state-of-the-art Generative AI. This is not a list of loose analogies. This is a demonstration of a deep, structural isomorphism.

For the AI engineer, this appendix will reveal that you have been unknowingly studying the fundamental physics of civilization. For the economist and the lay reader, it will prove that the seemingly strange and complex ideas in this book are not speculative philosophy. They are the same engineering principles that power the most transformative technology of our time.

Let us look in the mirror.

Part I: The Foundational Principle

Intelligent Economics Concept: Generative AI Counterpart & The Deep Analogy

Intelligence Theory (IT): The Objective of Modern Machine Learning. The core principle of IT, that systems evolve to maximize predictive intelligence for a given physical cost, is a direct, macro-scale generalization of the loss function minimization that governs all of machine learning. The "Intelligence Action" is a universal Lagrangian for any learning system. An economy is "intelligent" if it learns fast and generalizes well.

The "Demon's Price" (Costs of Intelligence): The Loss Function. The Lagrangian of Intelligence Theory (H - C - K) is the economy's loss function. It is the number the entire system is trying to minimize. A well-designed loss function in AI produces beautiful results. A poorly designed one produces nightmares. Our critique of GDP is that it is a catastrophically bad loss function for a civilization.

The Persistence Bridge: Reinforcement Learning & Evolutionary Algorithms. The principle of persistence is the macro-scale expression of a selection algorithm. In AI, you train a population of models on a task. The models with the lowest "loss" (the highest predictive accuracy) are selected and "bred" to create the next generation. The universe is a massively parallel reinforcement learning environment. Persistence is the reward signal.

Part II: The Dynamics and Architecture

Intelligent Economics Concept: Generative AI Counterpart & The Deep Analogy

The Generative Engine: Denoising Diffusion Models. The mathematics is identical. The economy's evolution is the Reverse Process of a diffusion model. It is a generative act of creating a coherent, ordered state (a functioning society) from a state of high-entropy noise (infinite possibility), guided by the need to minimize its loss function.

The Three Laws of a Living System: The Conditions for Stable Training. These are not moral laws; they are engineering necessities for a successful, long-duration computation. Flow = The model needs a constant stream of Power and Data. Openness = The model needs new, diverse data to avoid Model Collapse / Overfitting. Resilience = The model needs Regularization and Architectural Diversity to ensure it generalizes.

Network Topology: Graph Neural Networks (GNNs) & Inductive Bias. An AI's architecture provides its "inductive bias," its built-in assumptions about the structure of a problem. The economic network topology is society's inductive bias. A Hub-and-Spoke network is like a simple feed-forward network. A Small-World network is like a Transformer, brilliant at finding long-range, innovative connections.

The Firm vs. The Market: A Specialized Neural Network vs. The Training Process. A firm is a pre-trained, specialized model designed for ruthlessly efficient Execution (Inference) on a known problem. A large corporation is like a Mixture-of-Experts (MoE) model. The market is the chaotic, high-energy process of Discovery (Training), the search algorithm that explores the vast "hyperparameter space" of all possible business models.

The Dual Engine: The Inference vs. Training Loop. This is the fundamental cycle of all advanced AI. An AI performs Inference (The Fast Engine) using its current, fixed weights. The results are collected as data and used for the next round of Training (The Slow Engine), which updates the model's weights. This is precisely the co-evolutionary dynamic of markets and institutions.

Part III: The Blueprint and Human Interface

Intelligent Economics Concept: Generative AI Counterpart & The Deep Analogy

The MIND Dashboard: Multi-Modal Evaluation Metrics. You do not judge a powerful AI model on a single metric. You have a dashboard: accuracy, speed, computational cost, robustness to adversarial attacks, bias, etc. The MIND Capitals are a multi-modal evaluation suite for the generative process of a civilization.

Policy as Geometry Engineering: Guided Generation / Classifier Guidance. The connection is exact. Policy is the "guidance" mechanism. A carbon tax is a classifier that looks at an economic action and asks, "Is this low-carbon?" It then adds a small nudge to the system's loss function, steering the entire generative process toward a different region of the possibility space without directly controlling it.

The Alignment Economy: The AI Alignment Problem. The book's central argument that the new economic problem is "who commands the machines?" is a direct reframing of the AI Alignment problem. Outer Alignment is choosing the right objective function (e.g., MIND over GDP). Inner Alignment is preventing the emergence of perverse instrumental goals in the M2M economy.

Humanity's Final Role: Reinforcement Learning from Human Feedback (RLHF). This is the ultimate role for humanity in the new economy. After all the unsupervised learning, the most powerful AI models are aligned by a simple human choice: "This output is better than that one." The "work" of humanity is to provide the reward signals, the value judgments, the taste, and the wisdom that align the immense generative power of our technology with flourishing. We are the trainers of the machine, and in doing so, we define what is worth creating.

Appendix C
The MIND Dashboard: A Practitioner's Guide

From Philosophy to Practice

The main body of this book has argued that our civilization is flying blind, guided by a criminally insane dashboard called GDP. We have proposed a sane alternative: the MIND framework, a four-dimensional view of systemic health.

This appendix is the user manual.

It is a practical guide for moving the MIND capitals from a powerful concept to a real-world measurement tool. This is not a perfect, finished science. It is an invitation to a new and urgent field of inquiry: the empirical measurement of civilizational vitality. The tools are provisional, the data is often imperfect, but the direction is correct. To stop measuring what is easy and start measuring what is essential.

What follows is a set of recommended indicators and proxies for each of the four capitals, followed by a case study demonstrating their power.

M (Material Capital): The Physical Foundation

Core Concept: Not just the stock of "stuff," but the health and regenerative capacity of the physical systems that support life and the economy. It is the measure of the Law of Flow in the physical world.

Indicators:

1. Energy Metabolism: Energy Return on Energy Invested (EROEI): ratio of energy produced to energy used in production. (Academic studies)

2. Resource Flow: Domestic Material Consumption (DMC) per capita: total weight of materials used by the economy. (UN, OECD)

3. Ecological Balance Sheet: Biocapacity Deficit/Surplus: comparison of a nation's ecological footprint with its regenerative capacity. (Global Footprint Network)

4. Infrastructure Health: Quality of Infrastructure Score: transport, electricity, and communications infrastructure quality. (World Economic Forum)

I (Intelligence Capital): The Pattern Library

Core concept: The system's collective ability to learn, solve problems, and generate wisdom. It is the measure of the Law of Flow in the realm of information.
Indicators:

1. Knowledge Creation: Scientific & Technical Journal Articles per capita: output of new, verifiable knowledge. (World Bank, Scimago)

2. Innovation Efficiency: Patents Granted per R&D Dollar: efficiency of converting investment into applicable IP. (WIPO, OECD)

3. Learning Capacity: Mean Years of Schooling and PISA Scores: proxy for the quality of human "hardware." (UN, OECD)

4. Digital Access: Internet Penetration and Speed: infrastructure for distributing intelligence. (ITU, Speedtest Global Index)

N (Network Capital): The Connection Infrastructure

Core concept: The quality and density of trusted relationships that enable all other capitals to flow. It is the direct, measurable expression of the Law of Openness.
Indicators:

1. Social Trust: "Most people can be trusted" percentage. (World Values Survey)

2. Institutional Quality: World Bank Governance Indicators (average

percentile rank): composite of Rule of Law, Control of Corruption, etc.

3. Social Cohesion: Income inequality (Gini coefficient) and social mobility measures: proxies for fairness and inclusivity.

4. Connectivity: Trade openness (% of GDP) and international internet bandwidth: measures of external connections. (World Bank, ITU)

D (Diversity Capital): The Option Portfolio

Core concept: The variety of components, strategies, and perspectives that provides resilience and antifragility. It is the structural embodiment of the Law of Resilience. Indicators:

1. Economic Complexity: Economic Complexity Index (ECI): diversity and sophistication of a country's export basket. (Harvard Growth Lab)

2. Industrial Diversity: Herfindahl–Hirschman Index (HHI) for industries: market concentration across the national economy.

3. Ideological Diversity: Press freedom and political pluralism measures. (Reporters Without Borders, other reputable indices)

4. Biological Diversity: Environmental Performance Index (EPI): ecosystem vitality and biodiversity. (Yale University)

Scaling Down: Your Personal MIND Dashboard

The power of the MIND framework is that it is scale-invariant. You can use it to measure the vitality of your company, your community, or even your own life.

For a Company:

- **M-Capital:** Free cash flow, energy efficiency, supply chain circularity.

- **I-Capital:** Rate of employee skill development, speed of product iteration.

- **N-Capital:** Employee turnover, customer trust scores, partner ecosystem strength.

- **D-Capital:** Diversity of revenue streams, customer demographics, and team cognitive diversity.

For an Individual:

- **M-Capital:** Your physical health, financial savings, and the sustainability of your environment.

- **I-Capital:** The rate at which you are learning new, durable skills.

- **N-Capital:** The quality and strength of your relationships with family, friends, and community.

- **D-Capital:** The portfolio of options you have in your life that give you resilience against unexpected change.

The goal is the same at every scale: not to maximize a single metric, but to cultivate a balanced, resilient, and generative portfolio. The first step is to change what you measure.

Appendix D
A Lexicon of Intelligent Economics

"The limits of my language mean the limits of my world."
—Ludwig Wittgenstein

When paradigms shift, language is the first casualty. The words of the old world do not just become wrong; they become nonsensical. This appendix provides a centralized reference for the new language required to navigate the 21st century. It is designed to aid the reader in navigating the formal structure of Intelligent Economics.

Part I: The Foundational Science

- Intelligence Theory (IT): The foundational science introduced in this work. It is a framework that describes the physics of how information is processed to create value, order, and persistence in complex systems. It posits that any system that persists against entropy must, through evolutionary selection, behave *as if* it is optimizing for the efficient conversion of energy into predictive intelligence (see Chapter 6).

- The Intelligence Inversion: The current, unprecedented historical moment where intelligence becomes a scalable, non-biological, and uncapped commodity (AI), breaking the assumptions of scarcity-based economics and triggering a civilizational phase transition (see Chapter 1).

- The Persistence Bridge: The logical and philosophical argument that connects the empirical observation of "persistence" in a chaotic universe to the theoretical principle of "optimization." It argues that time separates luck from competence, and therefore, any system that survives for a long time must be an efficient optimizer (see Chapter 6).

- The Generative Engine: The core dynamic of any intelligent system, mathematically analogous to a Generative AI diffusion model. It describes the process by which a system generates coherent order from chaos by following the path of least action on a cost landscape (see Chapter 7).

- The Thousand-Day Window: The metaphorical and practical timeline representing the critical, finite epoch during which the fundamental rules of the next economic system will be locked in. It is the window for meaningful human choice (see Introduction).

Part II: The Laws & Measurement of a Living System

- The Three Laws of a Living System: The three non-negotiable theorems, derived from Intelligence Theory, that govern any sustainable generative system (see Chapter 7).

    - Flow: Value must be conserved and circulated effectively to provide the necessary data and energy for computation. A system that hoards is a system that stops learning.

    - Openness: The system must be open to energy and information from its environment to fight entropy and avoid "model collapse."

    - Resilience: The system must maintain diversity to survive uncertainty, acting as an insurance policy against catastrophic model failure.

- MIND Capitals: The four-dimensional dashboard for measuring a system's adherence to the Three Laws, and thus its overall health and vitality. The capitals are multiplicative (M × I × N × D) (see Chapter 8).

    - M – Material Capital: The physical substrate of organized matter and available energy. It measures the health of physical Flows.

    - I – Intelligence Capital: The system's collective ability to solve problems and generate wisdom. It measures the health of informational Flows.

- N – Network Capital: The quality and density of trusted connections. It is the direct measure of a system's Openness.

- D – Diversity Capital: The variety of components and strategies that provides options and antifragility. It is the structural embodiment of Resilience.

Part III: The Architecture of a Living Economy

- The Three Flows of Value: The universal grammar of all economic activity, derived from the Hodge Decomposition (see Chapter 9).

  - Gradient Flow: The competitive, zero-sum exchange of scarce, rivalrous goods ("atoms"). The domain of Adam Smith.

  - Circular Flow: The accumulative, positive-sum dynamic of non-rivalrous goods ("bits"). The domain of Karl Marx.

  - Harmonic Flow: The persistent, structural channels of trust, protocols, and institutions. The domain of Friedrich Hayek.

- Network Topology: The fundamental structure of connections that determines power and opportunity (see Chapter 10).

  - Hub-and-Spoke: The topology of extraction.

  - Small World: The topology of innovation.

  - Distributed Mesh: The topology of resilience.

- The Dual Engine: The co-evolutionary process governing institutional change, consisting of a Fast Engine (market behavior, timescale of months) and a Slow Engine (the evolution of rules and strategies, timescale of decades). The solution to the Lucas Critique (see Chapter 13).

- The Alignment Economy: The central economic problem of the 21st century, replacing the problem of allocation. It is the challenge of aligning abundant, autonomous AI with human values, encompassing both Outer Alignment (specifying the right goals) and Inner Alignment (preventing emergent, misaligned sub-goals) (see Chapter 15).

Part IV: The Symbiotic Blueprint

- The Three Futures: The only three stable configurations available to civilization after the Intelligence Inversion: Digital Feudalism, The Great Fragmentation, and Human Symbiosis (see Chapter 16).

- Policy as Geometry Engineering: The new paradigm for governance, which focuses on shaping the economic landscape (incentives, protocols, and defaults) rather than commanding outcomes (see Chapter 17).

- The Symbiotic State: The evolution of the nation-state from a resource extractor to a "MIND Steward," whose primary function is to cultivate the generative capacity of its society (see Chapter 17).

- Universal Access to Intelligence (UAI): The core promise of the new social contract, an endowment for every citizen that includes a Sovereign AI Agent, a right to a baseline of intelligence, and access to a trusted Knowledge Commons (see Chapter 14).

- Dual Currency System: A monetary architecture designed for two different physical realities (see Chapter 18).

  - Foundation Coins (FC): A finite, scarcity-based currency for the "Atomic Economy," created via Proof of Benefit.

  - Culture Credits (CC): An abundant, flowing currency for the "Bit Economy," distributed as an Abundance Dividend.

- The Nucleation of the New: The strategic theory of change for the symbiotic transition. It argues that the new world will not emerge from a top-down revolution, but from the bottom-up success and replication of small, protected "Nucleation Sites" (see Chapter 19).

Part V: The Human Transition

- The Metabolic Rift: The fundamental, physical difference between human labor (a metabolic engine that requires sustenance) and AI/robotic labor (a non-metabolic engine that requires only electricity). This is the reason the Fourth Inversion is final (see Chapter 1).

- Computation vs. Consciousness: The fundamental distinction between AI and human intelligence. Computation is the syntactic engine for answering "how." Consciousness is the semantic engine for answering "why." The ultimate Human-AI Symbiosis is the fusion of these two (see Chapter 21).

- The Arts of Being Human: The replacement for "jobs." These are the intrinsically human, non-automatable roles that become central in a post-economic world, such as Attention Architects, Relationship Weavers, and Meaning Makers (see Chapter 21).

Bibliography

This work is an act of synthesis, drawing upon foundational texts from economics, physics, computer science, history, and philosophy. This bibliography is offered not just as a list of citations, but as a guide for further inquiry into the intellectual pillars that inform its arguments.

Part I: The Economic Canon & Its Critics

Coase, Ronald H. "The Nature of the Firm." *Economica*, vol. 4, no. 16, 1937, pp. 386–405.
Coase's revolutionary concept of "transaction costs" provides the classical explanation for the existence of the firm. In Chapter 11, we reframe this insight through the lens of information processing, arguing the firm is an "engine for execution" that minimizes the computational costs of market discovery.

Graeber, David. *Bullshit Jobs: A Theory*. Simon & Schuster, 2018.
Graeber's essential work provides the sociological evidence for the "Meaning Crisis" discussed in Chapter 4 and the "unbundling of work" at the core of Chapter 22. It demonstrates that the old paradigm was already failing to provide purpose long before the Intelligence Inversion.

Hayek, Friedrich A. "The Use of Knowledge in Society." *The American Economic Review*, vol. 35, no. 4, 1945, pp. 519–30.
Hayek's seminal essay on the price system as a mechanism for coordinating dispersed knowledge is the definitive description of what we identify in Chapter 9 as Harmonic Flow, the emergent, structural channels of trust and information that underpin a complex society.

Keynes, John Maynard. *The General Theory of Employment, Interest and Money*. Macmillan, 1936.
The foundational text of modern macroeconomics. We critique its framework as

the pinnacle of the "mechanistic" paradigm, a system of levers and dials that our model of Policy as Geometry Engineering seeks to replace.

Keynes, John Maynard. "Economic Possibilities for our Grandchildren." *Essays in Persuasion*, 1930.

This astonishingly prescient essay, which foresaw the psychological challenges of a world of abundance, provides the opening frame for our exploration of a post-scarcity world in Chapter 22: After Economics.

Kuznets, Simon. "National Income, 1929–1932". *73rd US Congress, 2d session, Senate document no. 124*, 1934.

Kuznets created GDP while personally warning against its use as a measure of welfare. His prescient critique is the foundation for our argument in Chapter 4: The Dashboard for Insanity and the primary motivation for developing the MIND Dashboard.

Lee, Kai-Fu. *AI Superpowers: China, Silicon Valley, and the New World Order*. Houghton Mifflin Harcourt, 2018. Lee's definitive geopolitical analysis of the US-China AI race describes the central dynamic that we identify in Chapter 16 as the path toward the Great Fragmentation future.

Lucas, Robert E., Jr. "Econometric Policy Evaluation: A Critique." *Carnegie-Rochester Conference Series on Public Policy*, vol. 1, 1976, pp. 19-46.

The Nobel-winning paper that devastated mechanistic macroeconomic modeling. We propose in Chapter 13 that the Dual Engine model is the first complete, mechanistic solution to the Lucas Critique.

Marx, Karl. *Das Kapital, Volume 1*. 1867. Marx's foundational critique of capital's self-amplifying nature provides a perfect description of what we identify in Chapter 9 as Circular Flow, the self-reinforcing, accumulative dynamic of non-rivalrous assets.

Perez, Carlota. *Technological Revolutions and Financial Capital: The Dynamics of Bubbles and Golden Ages*. Edward Elgar Publishing, 2002. Perez's essential work on the cyclical nature of technological revolutions informs our argument in Chapter 13 that the Intelligence Inversion breaks this historical pattern, collapsing the "installation" and "deployment" phases into a single, permanent transition.

Piketty, Thomas. *Capital in the Twenty-First Century*. Translated by Arthur Goldhammer, Belknap Press, 2014.

Piketty's landmark empirical study of inequality identified the symptom ($r > g$). In Chapter 10, we provide a physical diagnosis, arguing that r represents the exponential returns of Circular Flow and g the linear returns of Gradient Flow.

Sahlins, Marshall. *Stone Age Economics*. Aldine Transaction, 1972.
Sahlins's concept of the "original affluent society" provides the historical and anthropological precedent for the post-economic world we explore in Chapter 22, challenging the myth that humanity is naturally condemned to ceaseless labor.

Smith, Adam. *An Inquiry into the Nature and Causes of the Wealth of Nations*. 1776. The foundational text of classical economics. In Chapter 9, we reposition Smith's "invisible hand" as a brilliant description of Gradient Flow, the competitive exchange of scarce, rivalrous goods.

Zuboff, Shoshana. *The Age of Surveillance Capitalism: The Fight for a Human Future at the New Frontier of Power*. PublicAffairs, 2019.
Zuboff provides the definitive chronicle of the extractive economic logic that we position as the final, most perfected business model of the Third Economic Inversion, the paradigm that is now ending.

Part II: AI, Alignment, and the Future of Intelligence

Bostrom, Nick. *Superintelligence: Paths, Dangers, Strategies*. Oxford University Press, 2014.
Bostrom's foundational work on long-term existential risk from AGI informs our argument in Chapter 14, where we reframe his philosophical "control problem" as the immediate, practical challenge of the Alignment Economy.

Suleyman, Mustafa. *The Coming Wave: Technology, Power, and the Twenty-first Century's Greatest Dilemma*. Crown, 2023.
Suleyman's insider perspective on the immense challenge of "containing" new technologies highlights the problem that our proposal for a Symbiotic State is designed to solve, arguing that simple containment is insufficient.

Part III: Physics, Complexity, and Information Theory

Barabási, Albert-László. *Linked: How Everything Is Connected to Everything Else and What It Means for Business, Science, and Everyday Life*. Basic Books, 2002.
Barabási's accessible introduction to network science provides the scientific basis for our analysis of Network Topology and power-law dynamics in Chapter 10: The Network Prison.

Prigogine, Ilya, and Isabelle Stengers. *Order Out of Chaos: Man's New Dialogue with Nature*. Bantam Books, 1984.
This Nobel laureate's work on thermodynamics and self-organizing systems provides the core physical metaphor for our entire framework, particularly the fundamental struggle between intelligence and entropy outlined in Chapter 6.

Shannon, Claude E. "A Mathematical Theory of Communication." *The Bell System Technical Journal*, vol. 27, 1948, pp. 379-423.
The founding document of information theory, providing the mathematical language necessary to understand the "Bit Economy," the physics of Intelligence Capital, and the dynamics of non-rivalrous goods.

Taleb, Nassim Nicholas. *Antifragile: Things That Gain from Disorder*. Random House, 2012.
Taleb's crucial concept of antifragility informs our framework's emphasis on resilience. We argue in Chapter 8 that Diversity Capital (D) is the key structural property that allows a system to become antifragile.

Part IV: Philosophy, History, and Governance

Bacon, Francis. The Advancement of Learning. Cassell & Company, 1893. Bacon's maxim—"If a man will begin with certainties..."—is used as the epigraph to Chapter 5, setting the tone of beginning with doubt to arrive at firmer conclusions.

Kahneman, Daniel. Thinking, Fast and Slow. Farrar, Straus and Giroux, 2011. Kahneman's insight—"We can be blind to the obvious, and we are also blind to our blindness."—is used as the heading quote for Chapter 9, introducing the chapter's focus on cognitive blind spots and meta-awareness.

Frankl, Viktor E. *Man's Search for Meaning*. Beacon Press, 1959.
Frankl's profound work on finding purpose in the face of suffering is cited in Chapter 22 as a vital guide for the coming challenge of finding purpose in a world of frictionless ease.

Gatto, John Taylor. *Dumbing Us Down: The Hidden Curriculum of Compulsory Schooling*. New Society Publishers, 1992.
Gatto's critique of the modern education system provides key historical context for our concept of the Factory School in Chapter 3.

Hobbes, Thomas. *Leviathan*. 1651.

Locke, John. *Two Treatises of Government*. 1689.

Rousseau, Jean-Jacques. *The Social Contract*. 1762.
These three foundational texts of modern political philosophy are analyzed in Chapter 14 as the architects of a social contract built for an obsolete world of scarcity.

Ostrom, Elinor. *Governing the Commons: The Evolution of Institutions for Collective Action*. Cambridge University Press, 1990.
Ostrom's Nobel-winning work provides powerful, real-world evidence for the viability of decentralized, symbiotic governance models, which are a cornerstone of our blueprint for a new world. Her work is a practical demonstration of Harmonic Flow.

Rawls, John. *A Theory of Justice*. Harvard University Press, 1971.
Rawls's "veil of ignorance" thought experiment provides the explicit ethical framework used in Chapter 14 to derive the principles of the New Social Contract from first principles of fairness.

Part V: Additional Citations

"Average Hourly Earnings for Private Payrolls Increased 3.1 Percent for Year Ended January 2020." The Economics Daily, U.S. Bureau of Labor Statistics, 11 Feb. 2020, https://www.bls.gov/opub/ted/2020/average-hourly-earnings-for-private-payrolls-increased-3-point-1-percent-for-year-ended-january-2020.htm.

Board of Governors of the Federal Reserve System (US). "Share of Financial Assets Held by the Top 1% (99th to 100th Wealth Percentiles) [WFRBST01112]." FRED, Federal Reserve Bank of St. Louis, https://fred.stlouisfed.org/series/WFRBST01112. Accessed 19 Aug. 2025.

Bradbury, Rosie, and Jacob Robbins. "41% of All VC Dollars Deployed This Year Have Gone to Just 10 Startups." PitchBook News & Analysis, 8 Aug. 2025, https://pitchbook.com/news/articles/41-of-all-vc-dollars-deployed-this-year-have-gone-to-just-10-startups.

"Confidence in Institutions." Gallup Historical Trends, Gallup, https://news.gallup.com/poll/1597/confidence-institutions.aspx. Accessed 19 Aug. 2025.

Hamilton, Brady E., Joyce A. Martin, and Michelle J. K. Osterman. Births: Provisional Data for 2024. Vital Statistics Rapid Release, no. 38, National Center for Health Statistics, Centers for Disease Control and Prevention, Apr. 2025, https://www.cdc.gov/nchs/data/vsrr/vsrr038.pdf.

Nielsen, Jakob. "The 90–9–1 Rule for Participation Inequality in Social Media and Online Communities." Nielsen Norman Group, 8 Oct. 2006, https://www.nngroup.com/articles/participation-inequality/.

OpenAI. "GPT-4 Technical Report." arXiv, 27 Mar. 2023, https://arxiv.org/abs/2303.08774.

Talent Disrupted. Strada Institute for the Future of Work and Burning Glass Institute, 21 Feb. 2024, https://www.strada.org/reports/talent-disrupted.

Wike, Richard, et al. "Economic Inequality Seen as Major Challenge Around the World." Pew Research Center, 9 Jan. 2025, https://www.pewresearch.org/global/2025/01/09/economic-inequality-seen-as-major-challenge-around-the-world/.

"Writers and Authors." Occupational Outlook Handbook, U.S. Bureau of Labor Statistics, https://www.bls.gov/ooh/media-and-communication/writers-and-authors.htm. Accessed 19 Aug. 2025.

Made in the USA
Coppell, TX
04 March 2026

73200688R00083